WORK LESS, FINISH MORE

PRODUCTIVITY LESSONS ON HOW TO SPEND
LESS TIME WORKING AND GET MORE DONE

MEGAN HOLSTEIN

"Work at your job and make a living. Work on yourself and make a fortune."

JIM ROHN

CONTENTS

Contact Me with Questions	vii
Preface	ix

UNDERSTANDING PRODUCTIVITY

1. What It Really Means to Be Productive	3
2. What Productivity Advice Is Actually Useful For	7

PART 1
6 PRINCIPLES OF PRODUCTIVITY

1. 80% of What You Do Doesn't Matter	11
2. Your Motivation Doesn't Matter	15
3. Your Willpower Doesn't Work	21
4. You Can't Multitask (Multitasking Is a Myth)	25
5. Big Achievements Come from Small Actions	30
6. Your Success Comes from Your Habits	34

BEING PRODUCTIVE

PART 1
FOCUS ON YOUR LIFE FIRST

1. Pick Your Priorities Carefully	41
2. Give up Pointless Activities	46
3. Stop Wasting Your Time	52
4. Maintain Your Relationships	60

PART 2
MEASURE WHAT MATTERS

5. Why You Need Objective Measurements	71
6. Decide Which Measurements Matter	75
7. Track Your Time	78

PART 3
TIDY UP YOUR LIFE

8. Become a Minimalist	85
9. Declutter Your Space	92
10. Design Your Space for Flow	102
11. Get to Inbox Zero	110
12. Break Your Phone Addiction	114
13. Optimize Your Computer	126
14. Optimize Your Browser	132
Conclusion	137
Liked the Book? Leave a Review!	139
Get Seeking Truth	141
About the Author	143

CONTACT ME WITH QUESTIONS

If you have any questions as you go through this book, feel free to contact me directly and ask them. This is not an attempt to gather emails, just a sincere offer to help. I check my email frequently and respond to as many reader emails as possible

Contact me directly at
hello@meganeholstein.com

PREFACE

The aim of *Work Less, Finish More* is to show you how to be truly productive. I want to show you how to take back your time so you can spend it how *you* want to spend it instead of having to spend it on work.

For that to happen, though, you need to be willing to spend some time making the changes this book recommends.

Much like how investing money in the stock market produces returns, using your time to make some changes to your life produces increased productivity that gives you all that time back and then some.

Some of these changes may feel pointless for you. If they are truly are pointless, then by all means, don't make them, but I encourage you not to leap to that conclusion. Give everything in this book a try, because I'm recommending it for a reason. If they don't work out for you, you can always go back.

Without further ado, let's get started.

UNDERSTANDING PRODUCTIVITY

"Amateurs sit and wait for inspiration, the rest of us just get up and go to work."

STEPHEN KING, *ON WRITING: A MEMOIR OF THE CRAFT*

1
WHAT IT REALLY MEANS TO BE PRODUCTIVE

> "Time management is about life management."
>
> IDOWU KOYENIKAN, WEALTH FOR ALL: LIVING A LIFE OF SUCCESS AT THE EDGE OF YOUR ABILITY

MANY PEOPLE MISUNDERSTAND THE PURPOSE OF PRODUCTIVITY advice.

At its core, productivity advice isn't about how to work longer hours. It's about how to get more out of the hours that you do work.

For example, consider two writers. Fred works 30 hours a week and publishes 12 articles a week. Steve works 10 hours a week and publishes 9 articles.

Fred certainly works harder, but it's Steve who is more productive. Steve gets nearly one article done an hour, and Fred gets less than half an article done per hour. If Steve worked as many hours as Fred, he would more than double Fred's output.

Productivity advice (at least, *good* productivity advice) is about being Steve, not Fred.

———

PRESUMABLY, everyone reading this book would like to be Steve. You would like to get more done in less time so you can focus on your health, family, hobbies, travel, or other non-work activities.

That's where productivity advice steps in.

Productivity advice teaches you how to get the most out of your working hours. How you choose to spend the rest of your time — whether it's on taking on more work, picking up an exercise habit, or learning to play the guitar — is up to you.

My passion for productivity skills comes from this freedom. I love having a free schedule to live life on my terms, and productivity skills enable me to break free of long working hours to live my life the way I want.

———

NOW THAT YOU know what it truly means to be productive, let's discuss two things people often *mistake* for productivity: busyness and workaholism.

Being Busy Is Not Productive

If you know someone who is never available to hang out because they are always busy, you know someone who is not productive.

Busyness is the opposite of productivity. A productive person does high-quality work quickly so they have all the free time they want. A busy person, on the other hand, never has free time. They take too long to get things done.

It's normal to be busy for a month or two at a time. Everyone has seasons of busyness in their life. But if you've felt overworked for years, you will enjoy this book.

Workaholism Is Not Productive

In America, we have a cultural notion of the always-on employee. This employee works ten hours a day and is still available on nights and weekends. They always update their JIRA board, get recommended for promotions, and win monthly company awards for performance.

They're available as a loving parent and spouse at home, of course, but only between "short" emails and "quick" phone calls.

We call this workaholism, and it's busyness made cancerous.

People feel good about themselves when they work hard. Accomplishing things is rewarding. Workaholics take this to the extreme. Like a drug addict, they overdose on the high of being productive and getting things done.

As workaholics add to their workload, they become less concerned with productivity. Productivity is about working fewer hours, and workaholics are not interested in working fewer hours. They feel good when they work *more* hours, not fewer.

Workaholism, then, is not about actual productivity. It's about feeling good. Workaholics use work to feel good the same way shopaholics go to the mall to feel good.

Like any addiction, workaholism isn't healthy. It unbalances your life, it eats up all your free time, and can paradoxically hold your career back.

NOW THAT YOU know what it actually means to be productive, you're ready to learn how to apply that knowledge.

2

WHAT PRODUCTIVITY ADVICE IS ACTUALLY USEFUL FOR

"My goal is no longer to get more done, but rather to have less to do."

> FRANCINE JAY, MISS MINIMALIST: INSPIRATION TO DOWNSIZE, DECLUTTER, AND SIMPLIFY

IF PEOPLE OFTEN MISUNDERSTAND WHAT IT MEANS TO BE productive, they definitely misunderstand how to use productivity skills.

Most people use productivity skills to get through tasks quickly at work. What motivates them to read books like this one is the desire to do more at work during their workday.

Doing more work is an excellent use of productivity skills, but it's not the only use. Productivity skills are useful for a wide range of things.

- Stay-at-home parents can use productivity skills to get housework and parental duties done faster.

- Students can use productivity skills to organize their coursework and learn more effectively.
- People planning long-term travel can use productivity skills to organize travel research and create a schedule.
- People doing home improvement can use productivity skills to reduce the amount of time and money a remodel will take.

Very few of my readers want productivity advice because they want to do better at work. They want productivity advice because they want to start a side hustle, pursue a hobby, or get fit.

My own interest in productivity skills stems from an interest in a holistic life. Productivity skills have helped me as a writer, but they have also helped me get fit, save money, and make the most of my time with friends and loved ones.

There are some things in your life you would like to accomplish. Perhaps you're a student trying to complete college online, or a stay-at-home parent whose responsibilities have multiplied. Or maybe you'd just like to finally start painting again.

It doesn't matter. If you'd like to get *more* done in *less* time, whatever it is, productivity skills can help you.

The next section is about how.

PART 1

6 PRINCIPLES OF PRODUCTIVITY

"Following conventional wisdom and relying on shortcuts can be worse than knowing nothing at all."

BEN HOROWITZ, THE HARD THING ABOUT HARD THINGS

1

80% OF WHAT YOU DO DOESN'T MATTER

"The secret of life is to get lucky and stay there."

CHARLEY ELLIS

ONE OF THE MOST UNFORTUNATE REALITIES ABOUT BEING productive is that most of what we do is a total waste of time.

Most of what we do is a waste of time because productivity adheres to a mathematical concept called The Pareto Principle.

The Pareto Principle

The Pareto Principle is a mathematical concept with roots in economics, computing, sports, biology, and almost every other field of human learning. It says this:

> "The **Pareto principle** states that, for many events, roughly 80% of the effects come from 20% of the causes."
>
> THE PARETO PRINCIPLE, WIKIPEDIA

The Pareto Principle is a universal mathematical truth. Across many areas of science, economics, mathematics, and human learning, the Pareto Principle holds.

- 20% of pea plants account for 80% of pea production[1]
- "Microsoft noted that by fixing the top 20% of the most-reported bugs, 80% of the related errors and crashes in a given system would be eliminated."[2]
- "In health care in the United States, in one instance, 20% of patients have been found to use 80% of health care resources."[3]

And for us, people looking to be more productive, 80% of our results come from 20% of our actions.

Only 20% of what we spend our time doing has a significant impact. The rest is a waste of time.

———

DON'T BELIEVE ME? Consider how much time you spend checking your email.

You only need to check your email once or twice a day to be effective. Yet most people do so dozens or hundreds of times a day. Anytime they have a down moment, they check their email.

And when they do, it's full of junk. Newsletters, spam mail, notes, you name it. These emails are a waste of time.

You waste all that time you spend checking your email on spam.

If you stopped checking your email so often and unsubscribed from all this junk, you'd free up hours of your time at little to no cost.

If you're clear on what matters to you and what doesn't, it's easy to identify your 20% and what is in your 80%.

There is what matters, like taking care of your family, taking care of your body, and pursuing your line of work.

Then there's what doesn't matter, like Macy's sales and video game weekend specials.

Tracking every election cycle polling change might make you feel like an informed citizen, but if you're not a political pundit or serious activist, chances are it's the 80%.

The truly productive keep a close eye on how they spend their time.

They know which activities are in the high-impact 20% and which are in the low-impact 80%.

When they see something from the low-impact 80% is taking up too much of their time, they either reduce the amount of time it takes or do away with it.

THE MORE YOU CUT OUT, the higher impact your time becomes.

When you cut the 80% that doesn't matter, you are left with the 20% that does — and then you add more things that matter, creating a new, *even higher* value 20%. You create a new 80% and 20% made up of higher-value activities.

In the end, it's impossible to cut out the 80%.

In this way, no matter how productive someone is or how essential they are to their team, the 80/20 rule is true for them. It's true for busy working moms. It's true for Fortune 50 CEOs. It's even true for the President. And even after you read this book, it will still be true for you.

Instead of trying to purge our lives of what doesn't matter once and for all, we need to learn to keep a watchful eye on everything we do.

Every day, we need to ask ourselves if what we're doing is in the 80% or the 20%. And if it's in the 80%, we need to minimize or cut it out.

In this way, we are continually creating new and higher-value 20% activities, pushing our productivity ever higher.

———

AS YOU MOVE through this book, it will reference the 80/20 rule again and again. Of all the lessons in this book, it's the most oft-repeated. But as you'll learn in the next chapter, it's not the only principle you need to know.

---

1. The 1 Percent Rule: Why a Few People Get Most of the Rewards by James Clear
2. The Pareto Principle, Wikipedia
3. The Pareto Principle, Wikipedia

2

YOUR MOTIVATION DOESN'T MATTER

"All the so-called "secrets of success" will not work unless you do."

JAYMIN SHAH

ONE OF THE BIGGEST MISCONCEPTIONS MOST PEOPLE HAVE about productivity is they think they need to feel motivated before they can start being productive.

Productive people know the truth: motivation is a *result* of working hard, not the *cause* of it.

Results don't care whether you are motivated. Results are results, regardless of how you feel while you earn them.

That results don't care about your motivation sounds like depressing news, but it's great news. After all, nobody ever feels motivated all the time.

Like any other emotion, motivation comes and goes. You may wake up some days full of motivation and wake up other days convinced the right thing to do is spend it all in bed.

If you depend on feeling motivated to be productive, you will always suffer from inconsistent progress. You will work hard to gain a mile one day only to lose it the next.

To make dependable progress toward your goals, you need to work consistently. Not just when you feel like it.

One of the most critical productivity skills you can learn is how to get started working and keep working when you feel completely unmotivated.

ANOTHER COMMON MISCONCEPTION people have is thinking they shouldn't force themselves to work if they're unmotivated because their work will suffer. They also think they will become more unmotivated.

If you are facing a task you want to do but just don't want to do right now, the best thing to do is acknowledge your lack of motivation and get started anyway. Once you get started, you will find your motivation returning.

Most people are familiar with this effect in the context of going to the gym. Many people dread going to the gym before they go, but if they decide to go anyway, they find they're glad they went. By the end of their workout, they feel excellent.

After a week or two of doing this, their body learns to associate feelings of pleasure with going to the gym. As a result, they no longer dread the gym. Instead, they feel consistently motivated to exercise.

We commonly think of motivation as a cause of work — "I will get started when I feel motivated" — but in reality, motivation is often the *result* of hard work.

The real challenge of motivation isn't getting motivated, but learning how to work even when you're not. If you master that skill, your motivation will grow naturally.

MY FAVORITE WAY of getting over that initial lack of motivation is what my father calls the "get up, dress up, show up" principle.

The "get up, dress up, show up" principle is based on what my father would say to me all the time when I was young.

"You need to get up, dress up, and show up," he said. "You can get there and decide you want to quit, but you can't quit from the bedroom."

When I was young and didn't want to show up for sports practice, that's what he said. "Get up, dress up, and show up." When I was older and didn't want to show up for networking events or career opportunities, that's what he said. "Get up, dress up, and show up."

And when I was finally old enough to think I needed to start going to the gym regularly, that's what he said too. "Get up, dress up, show up. If you don't want to work out, you can quit once you're there."

When I was young, this was just one of those things dad always said. It took on more meaning for me in my adulthood.

When I started to work out every day, I dragged myself out of bed at 6 AM, absolutely sure every day that I would turn right around and go home once I got to the gym. But once I was there, I always said to myself, "since I'm already here, I might as well enjoy the sauna..." and after enjoying the sauna, I said to myself, "I could walk a mile on the treadmill..." and after that mile on the treadmill, the idea of lifting weights seemed kind of fun.

I told myself every day I could go home whenever I wanted, but I never did. After a few weeks, I stopped even wanting to.

The beauty of this advice is that it's easy to put into practice.

It's daunting to tell yourself you're going to spend two hours at the gym lifting weights. It's not daunting to tell yourself you're going to go on a short car ride to the gym and back while wearing nylon shorts. It's not daunting to go spend fifteen minutes in the sauna either. It's not daunting to take a short run on the treadmill. It's not daunting to use one weightlifting machine one time.

You didn't have to listen to my father repeat the words "get up, dress up, and show up" ad nauseam for twenty-five years, but you can still benefit from his wisdom. Instead of making comprehensive commitments, just commit to giving yourself a chance.

- If you want to build a writing habit, don't commit to writing an entire chapter of your book every day. Just commit to writing two or three hundred words.
- If you want to fund your retirement, don't commit to saving one million dollars. Just commit to putting a little away every week.
- If you want to learn how to play the piano, don't commit to learning a complicated song. Just commit to sitting down at the piano and practicing for five minutes.

Whatever your goals are, commit to get up, dress up, and show up. After a few weeks, your motivation levels will skyrocket.

———

IT'S true that on some days, it won't matter what you do. You won't feel motivated. You'll drag your ass to the gym and do some light-and-easy exercises, but your motivation will still be in the gutter. You'll force yourself to write 1000 words, but you'll feel like each word is being dragged out of you.

If you've given motivation every opportunity to show up and it's *still* nowhere to be seen, I would recommend calling it a day and heading home.

If you force yourself to see a task all the way through despite hating every moment of it, you'll teach your body to associate *productivity* and *misery*. Over time, that attitude will cause you to feel miserable in response to the need to be productive.

Not a good thing.

Since most of us want to feel good while we're working, not terrible, I recommend you don't build this association.

Give your body every chance to see that getting things done is enjoyable. But if your body insists right now is not the time, listen to what it's saying.

Even now, my body sometimes tells me not to put in a full day. I never went home without working out, but some days I did find I could only lift for fifteen or twenty minutes instead of my usual hour and a half.

On those days, I didn't beat myself up about it. I went home without guilt, proud of myself for getting any exercise done at all that day. After all, some days be like that. All we can do is take it one day at a time.

SO IT DOESN'T MATTER how motivated you are. You still need to do the work. But that doesn't mean you should force yourself to do work when you don't want to work. Forcing yourself to be productive is a strategy that usually backfires.

If this seems like a contradiction in terms — it doesn't matter how motivated you are, but you shouldn't work if you don't want to — then the next chapter will clear it up for you.

3

YOUR WILLPOWER DOESN'T WORK

"How you do anything is how you do everything."

CATHERINE PRICE, HOW TO BREAK UP WITH
YOUR PHONE

YEARS AGO, I WAS DATING A MAN WHO SPENT A LOT OF TIME on his phone. *A lot.* He probably spent 5+ hours a day on Snapchat alone.

My relationship with the phone addict was around the time that Cal Newport's *Digital Minimalism* came out. Like many people, I was beginning to become conscious of how people overused their phones.

Spurred by Newport's book and the digital minimalism movement, I reconfigured my phone to be less addicting and discourage use. I did things like moving social media apps to hidden folders and downloading educational apps to use in place of addictive and destructive apps. (Later in this book, you will be shown how to do these things for yourself).

After a week or two, I showed the Snapchat addict my project. I explained what I'd been learning about how dangerous phone use was and that my phone changes would enable me to spend less time on my phone and more time focusing on what matters.

His response?

"That's good for you, sweetie, but I don't need all that. I have willpower."

He thought weaker people (like me) needed to rely on environmental changes to encourage healthy behavior for ourselves, but all that is necessary for people who "have willpower" (like him) is just to *decide* to change.

He may have thought that, but his willpower clearly wasn't working out for him, as his 8-hour-a-day phone habit made clear.

Many people approach self-control in this way. They see themselves as a tower of will, separate from their environment and able to make decisions about it at... well, *at will*.

The unfortunate reality is that we are not separate from our environment in this way. Everything we think, feel, and experience depends on what our environment around us is.

- We may not feel hungry until a nice, juicy steak or soft apple pie is served — then we're ravenous.
- We may not feel tired until we get home from work and sit down for the first time that day, only to fall asleep where we are sitting.
- We may not want to use social media... until we pull our phone out of our pocket and open it without thinking.

To make permanent changes to your life, you have to rely on more than willpower. You have to make it as easy as possible to accomplish your goals. You do this by changing your environment.

- If you want to lose weight, don't keep high-calorie food in the house. Buy a gym membership and put your gym clothes in front of your bedroom door.
- If you want to get more work done, make sure you have a clean desk ready for you whenever you want to work.
- If you want to spend more time with friends, block out specific times on your calendar and make plans with friends ahead of schedule.
- If you want to save for retirement, set your bank account to make an automatic payment every month.

In general, when you decide you want to achieve a goal in your life, ask yourself what would make it easier for you to achieve that goal.

What one-time change could you make that would make achieving your goal easier (or even automatic)?

In every case, make it as easy as possible for yourself to achieve what you want.

———

NOW YOU KNOW that the key to working when you're not motivated isn't to force yourself to work, but to make it as easy as possible for yourself to work.

But that doesn't mean anything goes. For instance, you can't watch TV while you work to make it easier on yourself. As we explore in the next chapter, multitasking is utterly destructive to productivity in all its forms.

4

YOU CAN'T MULTITASK (MULTITASKING IS A MYTH)

"Fucking two things up at the same time isn't multitasking."

DICK MASTERSON

Lots of busy, productive people say they rely on the ability to multitask.

They listen to a podcast while editing a marketing report, watch a YouTube video while performing company research, or conduct a chat with customer support in the middle of a meeting.

Often, multitasking seems like the only way to get through a busy day. But while it feels more productive, it is actually less.

What we commoners call multitasking, psychologists call rapid task-switching.[1] Like the name implies, it's the act of switching between performing one task and the other at high speed.

As any psychologist will tell you, rapid task switching is terrible for productivity.

The human brain evolved to single task on environmental stimuli: noticing food stores are running low, avoiding disease spreading through the village, fleeing a tiger in the bushes. When a human gives their full attention to something, the physical and mental feats they are capable of are incredible.

When we "multitask," however, we're not harnessing that full attention. As noted earlier, we are actually rapid task switching, switching between one task and the other at high speed. By the time we're focused on one task, we're already switching to the other.

As a result, we never truly focus on anything.

> "Multitasking does not in fact denote a quantitative enumeration of tasks, but a qualitative distinction between on- and off-task activity. In other words, multitasking is functionally equivalent to distraction."
>
> "MULTITASKING AS DISTRACTION: A CONCEPTUAL ANALYSIS OF MEDIA MULTITASKING RESEARCH" BY JESPER AAGAARD, SAGE JOURNALS

For some meaningless tasks, like chatting with customer support, full attention isn't needed. But to make a meaningful contribution at work, either through a meeting or report, or to create something new that's worth existing, we need to give our work our full attention. That means no interruptions, no distractions, and *no multitasking*.

The Longer You Single Task, the Better Your Results

It's better to single task, but not all single-tasking is equal.

To maximize your productivity, you want to achieve what psychology researcher Mihály Csíkszentmihályi calls a flow state.

> "In positive psychology, a **flow state**, also known colloquially as being **in the zone**, is the mental state in which a person performing an activity is fully immersed in a feeling of energized focus, full involvement, and enjoyment in the process of the activity. In essence, flow is characterized by the complete absorption in what one does, and a resulting transformation in one's sense of time."
>
> FLOW (PSYCHOLOGY), WIKIPEDIA

Everyone's felt flow before. At the very least, we felt it as children when we were outside playing with our friends, sticking our hands in the dirt and making mud pies. We felt it as young teenagers, reading our favorite books.

If we're lucky, we get to feel flow as an adult, pursuing our passion at work or developing our favorite hobbies at home.

Many of the great works of art created throughout the centuries were created by artists who learned how to harness flow states' power.

To maximize your productivity, you want to create an environment that allows you to start single-tasking and stay with it long enough to achieve a state of flow.

> "Humans are built for flow. We just have to design our environment accordingly."

Our environment allows us to enter flow when it is relatively free of distractions. The fewer distractions we have, the longer we can work, and the greater our ability to enter flow.

Therefore, your ability to enter flow depends on your ability to rid yourself of distractions.

When it comes to flow, there are two types of distractions:

1. Interruptions
2. Temptations

An interruption is a distraction that comes to you, like a spouse who keeps knocking on your home office door, a coworker who won't stop Slack messaging you, or incessant phone calls from debt collectors.

A temptation is a distraction that you gravitate towards, like the temptation to procrastinate by cleaning your entire house top to bottom or repeatedly pick up your phone to use social media while you're working.

To get the most out of your single-tasking time, you need to eliminate both of these distractions. To eliminate interruptions, put a sign up on the door that says "keep out!" and turn your phone to silent or Do Not Disturb.

To get rid of temptations, use content blockers, delete social media apps, turn your phone or internet connection off, clean your house before you start working, or do whatever else you need to do first. That way, when you start working, you're able to give your work all your attention.

ASKING someone to single-task on productive actions for long periods is a big ask, I know. But productivity experts know that sustained effort over many hours in one sitting is rarely ever as productive as a small, consistent effort over time. In the next chapter is why.

---

1. https://www.apa.org/research/action/multitask

5

BIG ACHIEVEMENTS COME FROM SMALL ACTIONS

"People tend to overestimate what can be done in one year and to underestimate what can be done in five or ten years."

"LIBRARIES OF THE FUTURE" BY J. C. R. LICKLIDER

FROM THE OUTSIDE, MASSIVE ACHIEVEMENTS SEEM LIKE THE result of enormous effort.

Accomplishments like starting a million-dollar business or writing a bestselling novel seem like the result of a Herculean effort, with more than a little luck thrown in as well.

Of course, they *are* the result of massive effort. But not the kind of effort with which most people are familiar.

When most people imagine working hard for a goal, they imagine working long hours with no breaks for eating or rest, studying well into the night, skipping sleep, and forfeiting a social life in single-minded pursuit of their goal.

If I tell you a student has to study "very hard" for an examination coming up, and you picture a student pulling all-nighters and mainlining coffee, you're picturing this type of hard work.

Truly productive people don't work this way. They can fulfill all their responsibilities and achieve incredible things, all while getting a full night's rest every night, taking regular breaks, and going home in the evening to socialize and spend time with their family.

They can do these things because they know the one rule of achievement:

A small, consistent effort is exponentially more productive than a flurry of effort all at once.

To explore this concept, let's imagine a writer who has decided they will finally write their first book.

Filled with excitement, he sits down every night for a week and writes 2,000 words each night, spending hours on his new project.

But after that week, he quickly loses motivation. His overwhelming work schedule swallows him up, and soon, he can no longer find any time to write.

Next thing he knows, a year has passed without him writing a single word.

Imagine if, instead, that writer made a small commitment to write a mere 200 words per day, which takes less than half an hour.

If he wrote 200 words a day, he would have 72,000 words by the end of the year — the length of a full book — without any special effort at all.

You can apply this principle to other areas as well:

- "If you need to lose 100 lbs, you might feel like it's hardly worth trying. But cut out 500 calories per day (the equivalent of a Mars Bar and a can of coke), and you'd lose one pound per week. After two years, you'll be at your goal weight."
- "If you want to run a marathon, but you're a bit of a couch potato, you can start by walking briskly for 10 minutes each day. By gradually increasing the amount you do, you could be running that marathon next year."[1]

The truly productive do not make work in fits and starts. Instead, they make a small and consistent effort over a long time.

Next time you want to achieve something meaningful, you shouldn't make a grand plan to put in four or five hours of work every day. That strategy will fail.

Instead, figure out what kind of small daily effort will move you closer to your goals, and put in that effort every day.

Don't fill your days with grandiose projects. Fill your days with consistent, dependable effort.

SUCCESS COMES FROM SMALL, dependable effort over time. This kind of effort can't be motivated by sheer willpower or a "feeling" of being motivated. It requires an environment that encourages that action. Add all of these things together, and you get a habit.

In the next chapter, we explore how truly productive people pull these principles together to build good habits in their lives.

---

1. These two examples, and the example of the writer from the preceding paragraph, are from "How a Small, Consistent Effort Lets You Achieve Goals You Only Dreamed About" on the website GetMotivation

6

YOUR SUCCESS COMES FROM YOUR HABITS

"We are what we repeatedly do."

ARISTOTLE

WE'VE DISCUSSED THE FOLLY OF RELYING ON WILLPOWER, AND we've discussed how big accomplishments come from small commitments.

Now it's time to put those together by discussing habits.

As anyone with a bad habit knows, a habit is a compulsion that doesn't require any willpower to engage in — in fact, it takes willpower *not* to engage in one.

And those compulsions are not to perform large, ambitious tasks, but to do little, mundane things. People's bad habits are habits like watching TV and eating snacks after work or letting the dishes pile up, not working diligently every day. No one has a bad habit of building spaceships in their backyard.

Habits aren't what you do when you feel good. Habits are what takes over when you're on autopilot.

When you are feeling unmotivated, what do you do? Those are your habits.

What separates productive people from unproductive people is their habits — whether their habits are good or bad.

Watching TV, snacking, and letting dishes pile up are bad habits. Brushing your teeth, reading every night, and checking your email every day are good habits.

Productive people are productive because when they are on autopilot, good habits take over. Unproductive people are so because when they are on autopilot, bad habits take over.

For productive people, their good habits move them forward even when they have no willpower of their own with which to do so.

For instance, I've built a habit of waking up at 6 AM and working.

While I was building this habit, waking up at 6 AM and immediately getting out of bed to meditate felt like dragging myself out of a warm cabin and into the tundra (I built this habit in an Ohio winter). It required *a lot* of willpower.

But after a few weeks, things changed. It stopped being difficult and started being effortless. It became a habit.

Now that I've built the habit, it takes no time or effort for me to wake up, get out of bed, meditate, and get some writing done. My morning habit has been incredible for my productivity.

The best part is, like all habits, it's a difficult habit to break; I wake up at 6 AM every day even in the absence of an alarm.

I want to meditate in the morning, even if I intend to take the day off.

And even if I take the day, week, or month off, I can pick this habit right back up again like I never stopped.

How You Can Build Good Habits

Habits — good, bad, or neutral — are built on *triggers* and *responses*. Something triggers the habit, like a feeling, scheduled activity, or time of day, and then your body automatically *responds*.

The feeling of being stressed *triggers* you to watch TV in *response*. The sensation of getting tired *triggers* you to brush your teeth in *response*. Waking up *triggers* me to go to my writing desk in *response*.

Building a habit is like dog-training for yourself. You decide on a trigger and a response and then expose yourself repeatedly to that trigger and respond appropriately.

Do that enough times, and your body will build the habit all on its own.

In the next section of this book, we will explore the kinds of good habits you should build and how to build them easily.

THAT'S the end of our discussion of productivity fundamentals. In the next section, you're going to translate these principles of productivity into practical changes in your life that will make you more productive and give you back your free time once and for all.

BEING PRODUCTIVE

"You're not meant to be anything. You just follow what you want."

HILARY FITZGERALD CAMPBELL,
EMOTIONALLY TAXING

PART 1

FOCUS ON YOUR LIFE FIRST

"Oh my friend, we're older but no wiser,

For in our hearts the dreams are still the same."

MARY HOPKINS, THOSE WERE THE DAYS

1

PICK YOUR PRIORITIES CAREFULLY

"Remember that if you don't prioritize your life someone else will."

GREG MCKEOWN, ESSENTIALISM: THE
DISCIPLINED PURSUIT OF LESS

ALL OF THE PRODUCTIVITY PRINCIPLES YOU LEARNED ABOUT IN the last section are integral to understanding how to be a productive person.

But if you use those principles to try to achieve everything, you're going to achieve nothing.

When we were in kindergarten, our teachers told us we were little balls of limitless potential who could do anything we wanted with our lives.

And they were right... sort of. We can do anything, but we can't do *everything*. We only have a limited amount of time — in this day, in this year, and on this earth. And once we're out, we're out.

Therefore, one of the most important productivity skills you can learn is to have focus.

Most People Aren't Focused

Most people don't have focus in their life. Their orientation is reactive. They take each day as it comes, doing whatever it occurs to them to do as it occurs. They follow fleeting emotions instead of a broader strategy.

My favorite example of this is the kind of entrepreneur who founds three startups at the same time. They try to build three billion-dollar companies simultaneously, thinking themselves Elon Musk — then they are surprised when all three of them fail.

You don't have to be a triple entrepreneur not to have focus, though. Stay-at-home parents can lack focus in their lives too. Imagine a stay-at-home dad who keeps starting projects around the house without finishing any of them. He doesn't have focus either.

To take advantage of focus in your life, you need to learn to say no to what doesn't matter and finish what does.

Another productivity mistake people make is putting other people's priorities first.

When their boss needs help at work, they're there. When someone asks for a coffee meeting, they say yes. When friends want to hit the bar, they're down. And when someone guilt trips them into doing something, they cave. (These people are called people-pleasers).

What they're doing when they do this is working on other people's lives before their own. Instead of prioritizing what matters most, they prioritize whatever happens to have their attention at the moment.

It's rewarding to prioritize the needs of others in the short term. You become your boss's favorite employee, you become your coworkers' most dependable teammate, and you gain a reputation as welcoming and helpful around town.

But in the long-term, it can sabotage your effort in your own life.

While you're busy helping everyone else with their goals, no one is helping you with yours. Your company never gets started, your book never gets written, and you never run your marathon.

Five or ten years down the line, you'll realize you've been busting your ass every day and have suspiciously little to show for it.

Productive people aren't people pleasers. They don't let others pick their priorities. They decide what's important to them and go after it.

That's not to say they don't make time for others — they do — but they make sure their most important activities get done first.

How to Cultivate Focus in Your Life

The obvious first step to cultivating more focus in your life is to decide what to focus on.

Sometimes what you need to focus on in life is evident. If you're an aspiring writer, it's obvious your most important activity is to write more.

But sometimes it's not so obvious. When your goals are obscure, or you don't know the best way forward, how do you decide which activities are the priority?

Deciding seems simple in theory. After all, all you have to do is make a mental choice. But when you ask people what is most important to them, most people have answers — too many of them. *My work, my startup, my dream of painting, my body, my family, my children, my golf game, my garden,* and on and on.

To drill down to what really matters to you, not just what you think matters, work backward from your dreams.

Picture your dream life. How much money you make, where you live, who you're married to, how healthy your body is, how you spend your time, all of it.

Now picture your life right now. What's different between your dreams and now? Those differences are where you should focus your energy.

For instance, my dream is to be a middle to upper-middle-class self-help writer digital nomad, who lives in their camper van, who is in excellent physical condition. So my priorities are building my writing career and income, building in my camper van, and taking care of my body. My daily goals are all oriented around writing, taking care of my health, and finishing my camper van project.

Once you know what's important to you, you need to learn to say no to what isn't.

Easier said than done. Many people have a tough time telling others no. They don't want to let people down, perhaps, or feel obligated to do everything their boss asks of them.

But if you want to achieve your dreams (or even just clean out the garage), you need to tell these people no. You can't let their priorities take up more time than your own.

It does suck to tell a friend you can't come to their party. It is difficult to tell your boss your schedule is full, and you have no more space for his side project. It's especially difficult when your boss starts guilt-tripping you into feeling like it's your responsibility to go above and beyond in this way.

But if you forfeit your time to their priorities, you will never finish anything. Your goals will be left unachieved, and years from now, you will still be right where you are.

To maximize your productivity and spend less time working, you need to learn to focus your efforts on your priorities first.

ONCE YOU SETTLE YOUR PRIORITIES, you're ready to begin making concrete changes in your life. One of the first changes you should make is to give up activities that don't support these priorities. Common examples of such activities and how to give them up are in the next chapter.

2

GIVE UP POINTLESS ACTIVITIES

"It couldn't last. Everyone was just killing time. But if all they did was kill time, time would end up killing them."

MICHAEL GRANT, GONE

SHALLOW, POINTLESS ACTIVITIES ARE ONE OF THE BIGGEST obstacles to most people's productivity, even though they don't know it.

A shallow activity is any recreational activity that encourages the user to enter a sedated, mindless state while they consume content of some kind. Shallow activities include Netflix bingeing, social media scrolling, video game sessions, and YouTube surfing.

If a recreational activity causes you to sit for hours and shut off nearly all the functions of your brain but the desire to consume more, it's a shallow activity.

At the moment, the pastime of most Americans is a shallow activity. Dozens of streaming services compete to bring us the latest and greatest opportunities to tune out in our living room. Video game streaming services allow us to experience video games anywhere, sometimes without even having to play the game ourselves. YouTube's autoplay feature enables us to lose ourselves in YouTube video after YouTube video.

Hours pass and the sun sets on the horizon, but we aren't aware. We are lost in a haze of shallow activities.

Why Shallow Activities Are Destructive

It should be immediately apparent to a sensible reader why these kinds of things are unhealthy in large quantities, but let's take some time to discuss their shortcomings in detail.

Shallow activities perpetuate themselves. Much like how doing drugs creates more desire to do drugs, consuming content mindlessly creates more desire to consume content mindlessly.

As you scroll social media more, you follow more people and have more posts to see. As you watch more Netflix shows, you need to keep up with more shows as episodes come out. As you play more video games, you have more games you need to finish. And on and on it goes.

They will continue to consume your precious time until you have none left.

Shallow activities affect your ability to create and think critically. It's a fundamental truth of neurology that the more you use an area of the brain, the more dense neural connections grow in that area.

When you sink into the mindless state of consumption shallow activities encourage, you are not strengthening brain areas associated with creation and critical thought.

You're strengthening areas related to consumption, which is why consuming only makes you want to consume more.

If you want to think critically, sharpen your argumentation skills, or even just retain the intellectual depth required to read a book, stay away from shallow activities.[1]

Shallow activities erode your mental health. Shallow activities, like social media and video games, have been linked with conditions like depression and anxiety.[2][3][4] While these activities may have positive effects when used in moderation (casual games, particularly, may help with depression)[5], using them for multiple hours a day does not bode well for your mental health. It's challenging to achieve your dreams when you're having trouble merely getting out of bed.

Shallow activities are physically dangerous. According to the Australian Diabetes, Obesity and Lifestyle Study, "every single hour of television watched after the age of 25 reduces the viewer's life expectancy by 21.8 minutes."[6] Someone who exercises and watches TV is at a similar mortality risk as someone who does not exercise and does not watch TV.[7] So even if you exercise regularly, your television habit is undoing all that hard work at the gym.

As if that weren't enough, researchers have discovered a strong link between screen time and poor sleep.[8] This link is strong regardless of what is on the screen at which you are staring. And of course, poor sleep is linked to a wide variety of things you don't want, like reduced functional IQ, heart disease, weight gain, and depression.[9]

Watching TV, playing video games, and even using social media can be beneficial in moderation. But if you spend more than an hour or two a day on these activities (according to the national statistics, most people spend far more[10]), they quickly become dangerous.

Why Deep Relaxation Is Better

I'm not trying to turn you into a 24/7 productivity machine. The American workweek is already too long, and I'm not interested in making the problem worse. Humans didn't evolve to be constant productivity machines. We evolved to live balanced lives, lives with work *and* play, effort *and* relaxation. To that end, rest and relaxation are critical to our well-being.

But most "relaxation" isn't relaxing. When people watch TV, play video games, or binge-scroll social media, they tell themselves they're relaxing, but they're not.

The thing about entertainment is that while it often superficially feels relaxing, it is neurologically not relaxing at *all*. It's a pipeline of ultra-high stimulation directly to your sensory cortices, a rainbow technicolor light show for your brain.

This sensory light show produces a sedative effect similar to that of the high of cannabis — you *feel* as if you're relaxing, but in reality, you're experiencing *more* stimulation than usual.

Ask yourself: When you realize you've spent the last 45 minutes scrolling Facebook, do you feel refreshed and relaxed? Do you feel revitalized, ready to take on your day? I'm betting you don't.

Back when I used social media, I certainly never did. After a social media binge, I felt something similar to a hangover —

a vague sense of feeling sick to my stomach, lethargic, and a little stupider than usual. Hardly relaxing.

False relaxation helps you press the pause button on life. True relaxation centers you, allows you to live in the moment, and helps you find peace.

And, of course, true relaxation is far better for you. Proper rest both stimulates your creativity and increases your productivity. In *Rest: Why You Get More Done When You Work Less*, Silicon Valley consultant Alex Soojung-Kim Pang explains that the most productive people are not those who spend a long time working or use clever productivity hacks, but those who make time for both work and deliberate rest.

His findings are research-backed and illustrated with stories from historical figures, both distant and recent. He explains why exceedingly simple restful practices like taking walks, naps, regular vacations, and having hobbies are critical to being your most healthy, happy, and productive self. (If you're looking for more on deep relaxation, I highly recommend his book).

IF ALL OF this has scared you a bit, then good. Chances are you have some shallow activities in your life that are keeping you from doing what you would like to do.

In the next chapter, you will learn how to identify which activities are the biggest waste of time and give them up.

---

1. The Shallows, Nicholas Carr
2. Lin, L.y., Sidani, J.E., Shensa, A., Radovic, A., Miller, E., Colditz, J.B., Hoffman, B.L., Giles, L.M. and Primack, B.A. (2016), ASSOCIATION

BETWEEN SOCIAL MEDIA USE AND DEPRESSION AMONG U.S. YOUNG ADULTS. Depress Anxiety, 33: 323-331. doi:10.1002/da.22466

3. Boers E, Afzali MH, Newton N, Conrod P. Association of Screen Time and Depression in Adolescence. *JAMA Pediatr.* 2019;173(9):853–859. doi:10.1001/jamapediatrics.2019.1759
4. Brunborg, G., Mentzoni, R., & Frøyland, L. (2014). Is video gaming, or video game addiction, associated with depression, academic achievement, heavy episodic drinking, or conduct problems?, *Journal of Behavioral Addictions JBA*, 3(1), 27-32. Retrieved Oct 1, 2020, from https://akjournals.com/view/journals/2006/3/1/article-p27.xml
5. Carmen V. Russoniello, Matthew T. Fish, and Kevin O'Brien.Games for Health Journal.Oct 2019.332-338.http://doi.org/10.1089/g4h.2019.0032
6. https://well.blogs.nytimes.com/2012/10/17/get-up-get-out-dont-sit/
7. https://well.blogs.nytimes.com/2012/10/17/get-up-get-out-dont-sit/
8. https://www.rallyhealth.com/health/screen-time-affects-health
9. https://www.webmd.com/sleep-disorders/features/10-results-sleep-loss#3
10. https://nypost.com/2020/04/14/average-american-streaming-content-8-hours-a-day-during-covid-19-according-to-new-research/

3

STOP WASTING YOUR TIME

"If what you are doing is not moving you towards your goals, then it's moving you away from your goals."

BRIAN TRACY

When asked, most people say they would rather hear the truth than a lie. Well, here's the truth:

Most of what you do with your time doesn't matter.

If you're like most people, you spend a lot of time just doing "stuff." You spend unstructured time picking up things in the house, checking email, watching YouTube videos, swiping absent-mindedly on your phone, and otherwise moving without purpose.

You also spend a lot of time on commitments that don't matter. You spend a lot of time in meetings, listening to other people talk while you click around your computer. You get on a lot of phone calls and go for coffee with people to have aimless, ultimately meaningless conversations. You spend hours waiting on flaky friends to show up.

The truth is, it doesn't matter if you ever fix that chair sitting in the garage. It doesn't matter if you ever go through those old boxes of shoes and donate some to Goodwill or not. If your house burned up in a fire tomorrow, you wouldn't ever miss them. You would save a lot of time if you admitted to yourself these things aren't important and chucked the lot of it in the garbage.

In the first section of this book, you learned about the 80/20 rule. Assessing much impact your activities have is one of the practical applications of the 80/20 rule; 80% of the stuff you spend your time on does not contribute much to your success at all.

In my last career, this was certainly true for me. In a previous life, when I was much better at wasting my own time than I am now, I was a mildly successful entrepreneur. My first successful company was a company that made apps for autistic children. We made a handful of apps, but at the time, the market for apps for autistic children was small. I'd seen the dollar signs, and I wanted a big market.

So, I started coming up with app ideas — dozens of them. I'd make a landing page and do some growth hacking to gauge interest in the concept for each one. It took around 5 hours per idea.

Not a single one of those ideas panned out.

You know why? It wasn't because they weren't good ideas. They were. It was because I wasn't interested in any of these ideas for their own sake. They were just harebrained schemes I'd dreamed up to make a quick buck. Because I didn't care, I didn't give any of them the focus they needed to get off the ground, and ultimately all I achieved was wasting my own time.

Three years of my life were wasted this way, on side projects and harebrained schemes I thought were the right thing to do at the time.

Every day, I see people making the same mistake I did. I see them deluding themselves into thinking they will fix that chair or contribute during meetings or start that app company. When they do not follow through, all they have done is waste their own time.

People who spend less time working don't do this. They are ruthless about how they spend their time. They want to work fewer hours, so they use the hours they are working effectively.

One of the most important ways they do this is by making sure they don't spend their time doing stuff that doesn't need doing.

Most people can only get one or two meaningful things done in their lifetime (if that). Pick something significant to dedicate your life to, and then cut out everything that isn't it.

How to Identify Stuff That Doesn't Need Doing

Once you accept in principle that most of what you do is probably a waste of time, it gets pretty easy to identify which things those are.

The number one indicator of a distraction is a lack of traction. If a month goes by and you don't do something you said you were going to do, chances are it's nothing more than a distraction for you.

Here are some everyday time-wasting activities:

Shallow activities. Per the previous chapter on shallow activities, spending any time on shallow activities beyond two or three hours a day is certainly something worth cutting out of your schedule. Start with social media, YouTube, and streaming services, which companies engineer to waste as much of your time as possible.

Anything around the house. Ever broken something and told yourself you would fix it, only for it to sit in the corner of the closet for the next three years?

It's time to stop telling yourself those stories.

If you have been telling yourself to repair that television, fix that chair, resell those board games, or modify your desk, admit to yourself you will not do those things because they are not worth your time and donate them to the local Goodwill instead.

Plans to learn a new skill or take up a new hobby. Learning a new skill is one of the great joys of life, and I completely support anyone who wants to do so. Having said that, when most people tell themselves they are going to teach themselves a new skill, they end up not doing so. For instance, many people tell themselves they will learn to play the piano, buy a piano, play it seven or eight times, and then leave it to take up space in the living room for the next nine years.

Don't waste your time telling yourself stories about how you will do things you clearly won't.

Clever hacks or quick ways to make a buck. I already told you my story about trying to make a buck by creating more apps. Other "clever" ways of making a buck include selling or reselling anything on Craigslist or eBay, thrifting and selling clothes online, or other seemingly effortless acquisition and resale schemes.

If you devote time to these things, they can become a thriving business, but if you only see them as a way to make a quick buck, you're never going to give them the time they need to be a thriving business venture. Best to focus your energy on things that matter instead.

How to Make Sure There's Time for What Matters to You

For some people, the idea that they do too much is news, but others don't need me to tell them they need to stop going to pointless meetings and stop pursuing side projects that aren't going anywhere. They already know they have too much on their plate.

When it comes to little commitments like cleaning out your garage or starting a side hustle, the only thing you need to do to get them off your plate is to drop them. But sometimes, your commitments come from others, and you can't just drop them at will.

When that's the case, what frequently keeps people from declining commitments is discomfort with telling people "no."

"I don't like to tell people no," they say. "I would rather just say yes to make people happy."

I confess I don't fully understand this experience. It's been a very long time since I've been afraid to tell someone no. Thanks to painfully extreme introversion in my high school years, I learned the skill of saying "no" to invitations to leave the house early in life.

That one little skill — telling people politely and firmly that no, I will not spend my time doing this thing they're asking of me — has contributed more to my success than any other personal skill.

The more successful you are, the more people want to suck up your time with coffee breaks and meeting requests. The more successful you are, the more critical it is you don't let them.

YOU MAY FEEL that going to get coffee with people is an important way of "giving back." But after ten years of people trying to "pick my brain" over coffee, the disappointing thing I've learned is 95% of the people who ask you for advice *will do nothing with it.*

They will happily spend three hours of your valuable time asking you question after question and studiously taking notes and then do nothing with the information. Ever. Five years down the line, they'll still be exactly where they were, still dreaming their dream.

And the remaining 5%? They don't need you to get coffee with them. They're proficient at using Google, YouTube, Medium, and paid coursework to teach them what they know. All they need is for you to point them in the right direction and warn them about common mistakes before they make them, which you can usually do via email.

Which brings me to my next point: It is critical to decline pointless requests for meetings and coffee and Zoom calls, but that doesn't mean you can't give back.

When people ask me for coffee, I decline them, but when I do, I send them a free copy of one of my books or links to articles they may find useful. To someone of the 5%, these resources will be a lot more helpful than a winding coffee conversation.

AS ODD AS IT SOUNDS, this skill needs to extend to your interactions with your boss.

Your boss's job is to manage you. But it's *your* responsibility to build a workday that is respectful of your time and maximizes your efficiency. If your boss is packing you into too many meetings and undercutting your ability to do your job, it's your responsibility to defend your time.

That means when your boss asks you to be at a meeting you know will waste your time, it's your responsibility to decline and respectfully explain to your boss why your time is better spent doing deep work.

If your boss values your productivity (which they probably will), they'll understand your point of view. They may make you attend the meeting anyway, of course, but they will at least understand where you're coming from and make an attempt to book you for fewer meetings.

YOU ALSO NEED to learn how to say no to any social event you feel pressured to attend. If you're getting an invitation out to a party, bar, or even a friend's house and you desperately do not want to go, you need to stand up for yourself and say so.

I've already mentioned how I learned the skill of saying no in early high school. As an extremely introverted teenager, I needed to say no to at least 50% of all invitations to go anywhere merely to survive the day without having a stress-induced crying jag. I cannot imagine how stressful my life would be if I didn't feel empowered to decline invitations to leave my house.

Learn to respect your own need for solitude. When someone invites you out to the bar, and your body tells you what you need is rest, respect your body by saying, "I don't think tonight is the night."

SAYING no and respecting your own time is essential to leading a productive life. And there is no area where respecting your own time is more critical than in your relationships. Read on to the next chapter to find out why.

4

MAINTAIN YOUR RELATIONSHIPS

> "This is the great trap of life: one day rolls into the next, and a year goes by, and we still haven't had that conversation we always meant to have."
>
> CHIP HEATH, THE POWER OF MOMENTS

For those who don't know, "toxic relationship" is a colloquial label for any relationship that isn't good for you. A toxic relationship is a friendship, romantic relationship, or familial relation that erodes your emotional health, ties up your resources, and drains your ability to live your life to the fullest.

While it's true that all relationships have their ups and downs, a toxic relationship is more down than up.

When thinking about your relationship with someone makes you depressed instead of joyous, you can be sure the relationship is toxic.

How Toxic Relationships Keep You from Being Productive

When a relationship is draining you of your energy and resources, you can't use those energy and resources to achieve your life goals. You have to spend your energy repairing the damage your toxic relationship causes — or even just staying emotionally afloat.

The damage toxic friends can cause includes, but is not limited to:

1. Using up your time on taking care of their problems (instead of spending your time the way you want)
2. Spending your money (in the form of excess expenses, guilt-trips, and personal loans that never get repaid)
3. Draining your emotional energy (forcing you to spend your time emotionally recuperating instead of pursuing your own goals)

People usually think of dropping friends as a mental health practice, not a productivity practice. But when toxic friends tie you up and keep you from pursuing your goals, you're not able to put time and energy toward the things that matter most to you. You're too busy coping with your toxic relationship.

How to Identify Toxic Relationships

The simplest way to identify a toxic relationship is to ask yourself how a relationship in your life makes you feel.

If it makes you feel exhausted, if it gives you a physical sensation of weight on your shoulders, or if it makes you say "ugh" inside, chances are it's a toxic relationship.

If you're the kind of person who likes sure signs, though, here are some sure-fire signs you can look for:[1]

1. Everything they say is about them. Every conversation is about their struggles, their problems, their accomplishments, or something about their life. Your life — your achievements, your worries, your romantic stories — never seem to come up.
2. They can't handle disagreement. If you disagree about something, be it over something as little as where to get dinner, they consider it evidence of a character flaw. The more serious the disagreement, the greater the character flaw.
3. They are chronically negative. They believe the world is miserable, nobody has a chance at achieving their dreams, everyone is a terrible person, so on and so forth. You can't remember the last time a positive word came out of their mouth.
4. There is always something going wrong in their lives. Whether it's a lost job, a wrecked car, a romantic disaster, or academic failure, there's always something. When you look at each thing individually, they seem like bad breaks, but taken together, you are forced to acknowledge the only thing these bad breaks have in common is your friend.
5. They are judgmental. No matter what the situation, they always have a judgment at the ready. Whether it's about how the stranger across the street is fat or

how your aunt is too well-off, they have something to say about it.
7. They frequently lie. Mostly about stupid stuff — whether they like a certain kind of music or food — but if they're willing to lie about the little things, they're probably willing to lie about the big things.

How to Heal Toxic Relationships

Many internet columnists preach about how you ought to cut toxic people out of your life as soon as possible. Personally, I don't love the idea of just cutting people out. As Luke Bryan sings...

> I believe we gotta forgive and make amends
>
> 'Cause nobody gets a second chance to make new old friends
>
> LUKE BRYAN, MOST PEOPLE ARE GOOD

So when you realize a relationship with someone is causing more harm in your life than good, I think you ought to try to repair the relationship first.

Here's how you do that:

First, clarify for yourself exactly what isn't working.

Get out a pen and paper and list every single complaint you have about the relationship, the person, and how they affect your life.

This note is just for you, so don't hold back. You can offer them sympathy and the benefit of the doubt when you talk to them, but here in private, be honest with yourself about what is and isn't working. (You can burn the paper afterward).

Some themes will probably emerge. Maybe everything troublesome about this friendship occurs at a bar, where it's easy to spend money and make mistakes. Maybe they cannot support your dreams or be an encouraging friend because they see themselves as a victim. Maybe there's something else going on entirely.

What's important at this stage is to identify what's going wrong *for you*.

Second, identify ways to fix this problem that don't involve confronting them.

It's easy to confront someone and tell them what they ought to fix about themselves, but that rarely produces any change.

Even if someone is amenable to working on their character flaws (which is a big "if"), calling them up one day and confronting them out of the blue probably won't trigger the personal growth you hope it will.

And anyway, it's not your job to fix your friends; it's only your job to love them.

So if someone has some flaws or behaviors that are hurting you, what can you do?

You can do the only thing anyone can do in this kind of situation: set boundaries.

If you decided what's damaging your relationship is your friend's cynicism, set boundaries around their negativity and enforce them.

You don't need to have a conversation with them to do this. All you need to do is enforce your boundaries when your friend crosses them.

When they say "that'll never work," say "that's what they thought about the moon landing." When they say, "people like us never get ahead," say, "that's what they thought about Barack Obama." You might find they become more positive as well.

If you decided your friend's bar-going habits cause you a problem, defend your boundaries by suggesting you do other things together instead.

Next time they ask to go to a bar, suggest you visit a local bookstore or coffee shop instead. When they ask if you want a drink, say, "Nah, I'm not in the mood for beer today," even if you are. Create situations with that friend that will forge a new, healthier friendship in place of the old one.

Setting boundaries won't heal a toxic relationship overnight. In fact, it will probably make the relationship *worse* for a little while. You have upset the status quo.

It will take a month or two before a new status quo settles in. When it does, you will begin to see the positive changes you're looking for.

Make sure to stick with it long enough for that to happen.

Third, if nothing else works, confront them.

You can't solve every problem by working on your half of the relationship. If someone owes you thousands of dollars they haven't paid back, for instance, and it's driving a wedge between you, there's pretty much nothing you can do other than talk to them about it.

Other times, working on your half doesn't produce the change you need. You've been trying positivity with your cynical friend for five months now, and instead of seeing this as an opportunity to be more positive, she gets angry at you. You're asking your bar friend out to play kickball and cook dinner with you, but he either shows up with a six-pack or decides to go to the bar anyway. Having a frank conversation is the only option you have left.

Many people approach conversations with these intending to change the person they're confronting. *This will not work.* The only person who can change someone is themselves.

All you can achieve in this conversation is to make clear what you want and see if the other person is willing to do that. Either they are, or they aren't.

Here's how you should approach that conversation:

- Keep it about yourself. Instead of pointing out their flaws ("You're so cynical"), talk about the environment you're trying to create for yourself ("I'm trying to create a positive environment that enables me to aim higher"). Psychologists call this using "I"-statements.
- Ask them what they want for themselves. If your bar friend wants to stop going to the bar so often as well, he might be interested in doing other activities once you point out he doesn't. But if he's OK with his life and thinks you've become stuck-up or judgmental, it doesn't matter what you say; he will do what he will do.
- If there's a problem that's holding them back, such as unemployment, personal loans, a gambling problem, so on and so forth, ask them what they're

going to do about it. If they answer with generalities ("I'm working on it") instead of specifics ("I'm going to meetings"), assume it's not going to get any better in the future.

If my previous experience is any indicator, it's usually pretty clear where their head is after about twenty minutes. Either they weren't aware of how their behavior affected their relationship with you, and they're interested in what you have to say, or they feel defensive because they think they are fine the way they are and that it's *you* who has the problem.

In a way, they're right. If they're OK with themselves the way they are, it *is* you who has the problem.

If this is how they feel, then you are left with a choice to make.

What to Do If You Are on Your Own

Going through the conflict-resolution strategies above can put things back on the right track with people who have hit a rough patch in their life.

But the most unhealthy relationships — ones with people who have major character flaws that manifest as serious issues like financial irresponsibility, drug addiction, and chronic excuse-making — are immune to these repairs. With these relationships, the only way to stop the bleeding is to pull out the knife.

Next time your toxic friend wants to spend time with you doing something unhealthy, and they reject all your attempts at a more constructive relationship, tell them...

- "That's not something I can do."

- "I appreciate the offer, but I'm trying to [change my life in this way]."
- "I'm glad you thought of me, but I don't want to talk about [negative thing] anymore."

Make sure to leave the door open behind you. Let your cynical friend know that while you can't be around negativity anymore because you've decided to take your life in a different direction, the door is always open to her if she wants to try a more positive kind of lifestyle. Let your alcoholic friend know if he ever wants to see more of life than the local clubs and bars, you're just a phone call away. Nothing weighs on you more than a door you've shut forever.

YOU'VE REACHED the end of this section, and by now, you've taken thorough stock of your life. You've decided your priorities, given up time-wasting activities, and healed your relationships. All of this has created a great deal of free time in your life.

Next comes being even more productive with your working time to create more free time in your life.

In the next section, you're going to take the first step to increase your productivity by taking stock of your current productivity level and using the principles you learned earlier to identify ways to improve.

---

1. The following list is adapted from a list available on Science of People called "7 Types of Toxic People and How to Spot Them." (https://www.scienceofpeople.com/toxic-people/)

PART 2

MEASURE WHAT MATTERS

"The life of every man is a diary in which he means to write one story, and writes another; and his humblest hour is when he compares the volume as it is with what he vowed to make it."

J.M. BARRIE

5

WHY YOU NEED OBJECTIVE MEASUREMENTS

"What's measured, improves."

PETER DRUCKER

In our discussion of the Pareto Principle, we ended by saying that the genuinely productive are always on the lookout for high-impact and low-impact activities.

But to identify which activities are high-impact and which are low-impact, you need to know what the impacts of your actions *are*.

Measuring productivity is another area of productivity where human bias crops up and causes all kinds of problems. In this case, our biases do not allow us to see objectively how effective our efforts are. Our instinct is to equate *how hard we feel we've worked* with how productive we've been.

That instinct gets us in trouble. Suppose we measure our productivity by how hard we feel we've been working. If we do, we will respond to unsatisfying productivity levels by doubling down on what isn't effective by working ourselves even harder. We'll overwork ourselves without being any more productive.

We need a way of assessing our productivity levels that isn't tied to our subjective estimation of how hard we've been working. An *objective* way.

An objective way of assessing the effectiveness of our efforts has two components:

1. Measuring our effort (time and money spent)
2. Measuring the results of our effort (objective results)

People with productivity skills track both of these things, and then they regularly review their stats to see how they could maximize their results while minimizing their efforts.

Let's take a look at what this looks like for a writer.

Writing is a career in which it's relatively easy to assess one's productivity independent of how hard one feels they work. We writers can assess our efforts via time-tracking software, software that logs all the time we spend writing, and we can assess our results in terms of words written per hour or per day, articles published per week or month, or books published per month or year.

If we find we're spending a lot of time in front of the computer but not very many words are being written, we can learn how to write faster. If we find we're not spending much time writing in the first place, we can make changes that ensure we'll spend more time writing.

Like the productive writer, productive people measure their effort and its results to figure out their best opportunities for improvement.

MEASURING our efforts also helps us find our lost time.

Lost time is my name for that time we spend without realizing we spent it. You know that feeling when you look at the clock and realize, "oh my God, it's already 6 PM, and I still haven't done X/Y/Z?!" that is the feeling of lost time.

Earlier, we discussed the idea that most of what you spend your time on isn't worthwhile. Well, we often don't consciously choose to spend our time that way; we do it because we've lost that time.

Measuring what matters is how you find lost time. When you're tracking your time and where it goes, you know just how long you spend doing this or that. When you know where your time is going, you can make mindful decisions about whether you want to spend your time the way you're spending it. When you don't know, you're just guessing.

WHAT'S *MOST* interesting about tracking your time is that even the mere act of tracking your time makes you more efficient about how you spend your time, even if you don't set any goals or do any further assessment.

Merely tracking our time makes us more efficient because of a neat psychological trick: When we record our progress on something, the mere act of recording progress makes us more apt to progress. Scientists have found this to be true for weight loss; participants in weight loss programs lost more weight if they self-monitored their progress.[1]

While researchers have done no longitudinal studies on the effect of self-monitoring time spent, productivity experts and career coaches have long been aware of the effect personal time tracking has on productivity levels.

———

AS YOU CAN SEE, there is immense value in tracking your own time. But you can't just track everything, or you'll end up wasting your own time with all the tracking. Learn how to identify what to track and how to track it effectively in the next chapter.

---

1. Self-Monitoring in Weight Loss: A Systematic Review of the Literature, Lora E. Burke PhD, MPH, Jing Wang PhD, MPH, RN, Mary Ann Sevick ScD, RN (https://www.sciencedirect.com/science/article/abs/pii/S0002822310016445#!)

6

DECIDE WHICH MEASUREMENTS MATTER

"It is not that we have a short time to live, but that we waste much of it."

SENECA, ON THE SHORTNESS OF LIFE

Now that you know how important tracking your success is, it's time to decide *what* you should be tracking.

In a world bursting at the seams with data, it's easy to think we should be collecting and analyzing as much data as possible, but that's not the case. According to the Pareto Principle, 20% of our trackable information will predict 80% of our results (yes, it applies here too). So instead of trying to track everything you can, track only what is predictive of success.

A metric is predictive of success if there is a direct relationship between that metric and the success you experience.

As a blogger, the number of articles I publish per week is predictive of success. If I post 0 articles on a given week, I know I'm not going to be successful that week! While posting a higher number of articles per week does not guarantee success, posting more gives me more opportunities to succeed. After all, I can't have an article go viral this month if I have published no articles.

Many writers make the same mistake here. Instead of tracking the number of articles they write, they track the number of words they write.

As a writer, I know how good it feels to write a lot of words. But if I write a lot of words but do not publish any articles, I will not be successful. To find success as a writer, I need to publish, not just write.

Choose metrics because they predict your success, not because they make you feel good.

In the business world, these metrics are called Key Performance Indicators, or KPIs for short. Businesses closely monitor their KPIs to see how they are doing in the marketplace. People who want to be productive closely monitor their KPIs to see how productive they are with their time. The higher their productivity per hour, the fewer hours they have to work.

A typical example of a KPI most people want to track is their weight. People track their weight because they want to make sure their body fat percentage stays below a certain point. While weight is not the best KPI for monitoring body fat percentage,[1] it is a reasonably good metric that is also easy to track.

Which brings me to my next point: Make sure you pick a metric that's easy to track.

One of the easiest ways to mess up tracking your progress is to pick a KPI that's difficult to track. For instance, if you want to measure your body fat percentage, you can track your progress by taking arm, waist, hip, and leg measurements every day and plugging them into a body fat percentage calculator... or you could just look at your weight at the end of the day a few times a week.

On a related note, make sure your KPI's are easy to record as well.

A great example of a KPI that's easy to record is my screen time. My time-tracking software RescueTime automatically captures all my screen time for me. Everything I do on my computer throughout the week — write, read, edit, play games, watch YouTube — is all recorded for me automatically by RescueTime. It costs me nothing to record the information, and it is always there for me to view.

Most KPI's will not be as easy to record. To record the number of articles you write per week, you will likely need to keep a spreadsheet with the numbers. You will need a health app to record your weight. But the small amount of overhead required to track a KPI will be well worth it when you can see your progress in real-time.

NOW YOU KNOW why tracking matters and what you should track. In the last chapter of this section, you'll learn that tracking your own time can be as easy as setting up a few pieces of software to do it all for you automatically.

---

1. Health At Every Size by Linda Bacon, (https://amzn.to/3ovPUNE)

7

TRACK YOUR TIME

"You may delay, but time will not, and lost time is never found again."

BENJAMIN FRANKLIN

Now that you know the importance of tracking your metrics, I want to go over why you should track your time.

Everyone's different. Our productivity goals are different, our skills are different, and the amount of resources we have at our disposal is different. One thing we all have in common, though, is time. Everyone, from the richest man to the poorest, has the same 24 hours in their day.

How we use our time can make the difference between wasting our lives and spending them doing something meaningful.

But thanks to our human biases, the 80/20 rule, and faulty beliefs about willpower, most of us waste much of it.

The most powerful thing you can do to ensure you don't waste your time is to track it. And thanks to digital technology and software, doing so is easier than ever.

How to Track Your Time

Some people track every hour, half-hour, or even fifteen-minute increment in their lives. While I have no doubt this provides them with valuable information about how they spend their time, it takes pretty serious dedication to maintain.

I've never been able to summon this kind of dedication in myself, and if I, *a self-help writer*, can't summon the dedication for a complicated self-help hack, I doubt my readers can either.

This entire book's end goal is to help you get more productive so you can spend less time working. If a time-tracking system introduces more work into your day than it saves, it's not helpful.

Instead, I rely on automated time trackers. I install time trackers on all my devices — my computer, phone, tablet, workout equipment, ebook reader, or anything that will automatically track my time.

The goal of tracking your time is not to make sure you're always working. That's tremendously unhealthy. The purpose of tracking your time is merely to gain insight into how you spend your time. This insight keeps us from deluding ourselves into believing we spend a lot of time working when really, we spend a lot of time browsing Instagram.

The funny thing is, once you have insight into how you spend your time, you start spending your time more effectively. Like dogs shown their mess, people shown their failures are more likely to correct them — even when we're just showing ourselves.

How to Install Time Trackers

There are some free and easy to install time trackers for your computer, smartphone, and tablets. It takes a few days to collect enough data to work with, so stop and set them up now. That way, your data will be ready when you are.

- Phone/Tablet Time Trackers: Screen Time (iPhone)[1] | RescueTime[2]
- Desktop Time Trackers: RescueTime[3]

How to Review Your Time

Reviewing your time is fairly easy. Go back over your personal KPIs and look up the data you've recorded on them. Compare them to the real data you have from your devices and what you've achieved during the week.

- Did you meet the goals you wanted to meet?
- If not, consider why. Keep reading this book to learn about changes you can make that will enable you to meet your goals.
- If you did, what allowed you to do so? Recall the 80/20 rule, and double down on whatever made you productive.

THERE'S ONLY one more section in this book, but the end of this chapter is an excellent place to stop for a day or two. Time trackers are a potent productivity tool, but only if you give them some time to do their job.

In the next section, you'll use these time trackers to inform some powerful practical interventions in your life that will increase your productivity and give you back tons of free time.

---

1. https://support.apple.com/en-us/HT208982
2. https://www.rescuetime.com/rp/meholstein
3. https://www.rescuetime.com/rp/meholstein

PART 3

TIDY UP YOUR LIFE

"What you are surrounded by all day influences you more than you think."

AUTHOR UNKNOWN

8

BECOME A MINIMALIST

"The things you own end up owning you."

CHUCK PALAHNIUK, FIGHT CLUB

MOST PEOPLE I MEET NEED A DOSE OF MINIMALISM, EVEN IF they don't realize it.

When the topic of minimalism comes up in my personal life, most people tell me they're "not a minimalist, but not really into possessions either." That would be a nice sentiment if it were true — but based on what I observe, it isn't. The same people who say this to me not only fill their closet with clothes until it bursts, but also fill a dresser and perhaps an armoire or storage unit with clothes until *they* burst as well.

Many Americans keep going, filling under-bed bins and external storage units with clothes with "off-season" clothes they never manage to wear even when it's the on-season.

To say nothing of the rest of an American's possessions: plastic bins filled with broken airsoft guns and ten-year-old camouflage shoved in the closets of men who haven't been airsofting in over a decade, piles and piles of random paperwork littering the corners of home offices, and entire garages filled with random bins and abandoned power tools — garages so full they no longer have enough room for cars in the first place.

We Americans need less than ten percent of what we use. Most Americans own so many clothes they rent storage units for them, but at the same time, we wear no more than twenty to thirty articles of clothing regularly. (To see which clothes these are for you, look in the laundry bin and on the floor. The clothes you see there are the ones you wear.)

Many Americans own sports equipment for all kinds of random sports they have only played once in the last five years. Many more Americans own bins and bins of random cables, components, and tools, telling themselves they'll "sort through that stuff one day."

If we want to be productive, we need to admit "one day" will never come. We need to 80/20 our possessions and clear out some space for our new, productive lives.

Here are some reasons why:

Reason #1: Minimalism Reduces Decision Fatigue

The primary reason billionaires, executives, and other well-to-do people adopt minimalism is that it reduces *decision fatigue.*

Decision fatigue is that curious condition most often experienced at the end of the day when you want people to *stop asking you questions.*

> *In decision making and psychology, decision fatigue refers to the deteriorating quality of decisions made by an individual after a long session of decision making. It is now understood as one of the causes of irrational trade-offs in decision making. For instance, judges in court have been shown to make poorer-quality decisions late in the day than they do early in the day. Decision fatigue may also lead to consumers making poor choices with their purchases.*
>
> WIKIPEDIA, DECISION FATIGUE

Minimizing decision fatigue is one of the top priorities of anyone looking to maximize their performance. For this reason, Barack Obama and Mark Zuckerberg wear the same thing to work every day. If they wear the same thing to work every day, that's one more thing they don't have to decide.

Personal possessions are the enemy of people who fight decision fatigue because each thing you possess multiplies the number of decisions you must make.

If you own one outfit, there's no decision to make. If you own five, you're choosing between five outfits every morning. If you own fifty, you're choosing from *fifty* outfits every morning. Own enough clothes and hygiene products, and getting ready for the day can become a project unto itself.

It works the same way for everything else you own. If you own a small house, a reading chair, a desk for working, a kitchen, and a bed, then when you get home from work, all you have to do is ask yourself if you'd like to read, work, cook, or sleep. If you own a three thousand square foot house with all kinds of stuff bursting out of every room, the number of options you have is staggering.

In this way, everything you own costs energy. You must make decisions about it and account for it, and navigate around it. To eliminate decision fatigue, you need to decide which of these items is worth that cost.

Reason #2: Minimalism Saves You Money

This stereotype about minimalism is true. People who buy and own fewer things tend to spend less money on those things.

Some of how minimalism saves me money is obvious. I'm no longer spending $2000 a year on clothes from designer clothing shopping sprees. Nor am I paying $2000 for the latest and greatest laptop, tablet, or phone every year. And since I became a minimalist before becoming financially powerful enough to buy a car, I will never have to pay $10,000 for the privilege of driving a car off of a lot.

Some of how minimalism saves me money is not so obvious. For instance, used cars are not only cheaper when you purchase them, but they also have more affordable car insurance premiums.

They are also less costly to repair. I recently paid $1000 to have the entire heavy-duty front brake assembly on my 2009 Ford E250 replaced; my mom recently had to pay $1000 just for a new 'backup proximity sensor' on her recently produced minivan. God only knows how much it would be for her to get her brake assembly replaced.

Speaking of automotive costs, since I'm running fewer errands and going to fewer places to buy fewer things, I spend less on gas. (Even with that E250).

Minimalism also saves me money on rent. With fewer things to own, I need less space for my home to feel spacious. Requiring less space dramatically increases the number of housing options available to me — smaller apartments are nearly always cheaper and easier to find.

These reduced costs have given me the financial flexibility I need to pursue writing as a career. If I were not a minimalist, I have no doubt I would need to keep a full-time job in project management or something similar to make ends meet. Thank God, I don't.

Reason #3: Minimalism Saves You Time

Time savings isn't a benefit of minimalism I see discussed as much by other people, but it's easily my favorite thing about minimalism. When you own less and buy less, you have more free time.

Minimalism saves me time because minimalists spend less time shopping.

Shopping used to be my idea of a good time. When I was younger, a friend of mine and I would spend entire days at local malls, department stores, and discount warehouses, coming home with large bags full of lovely things we bought that day.

We told ourselves we "needed" these things because people we wanted to be like on Instagram and Tumblr had them, but that was patently untrue. We just wanted them. And anyway, we had a blast getting them.

Now that I'm a minimalist, shopping is a pain in the ass to me. I am lightning fast when running errands. I can be in and out of a big box shop in seven minutes. I have even unlocked the mystical ability to go to the grocery store while hungry and not buy the entire store.

My boyfriend, who is not a minimalist, tells me I am tyrannical in my hatred of visiting stores. I'm okay with that. When I'm on my deathbed, I'm not going to wish I'd spent more time in stores.

Minimalism also saves me time because it spares me prep time around the house.

People always mention that being a minimalist makes it easier to clean, but they forget to explain why it's important to clean.

We don't clean our houses because God told us to and we're going to get a slap on the wrist if we don't; we clean our houses because it's easier to live in a clean house.

I did not grow up in a clean house. Doing anything in my parent's house was proceeded by a prep time of anywhere from fifteen minutes to an hour, during which I had to find somewhere to make space to do what I wanted and search the house top-to-bottom for the materials for what I wanted to do (or run to the store to buy them if I could not find them). As a result, I didn't do much that I couldn't do in my own bedroom space.

I don't have that problem as an adult. As a minimalist, I don't own much stuff. Because I don't own much stuff, my space in the house is typically quite clean. Because my space in the house is quite clean, it is easy for me to decide I want to spend the day working, trying my hand at watercolor painting again, or attempting to cook. I never have to clean up, make space, find things, or put things away. My watercolors are right there on the shelf and my desk is already clean, so I can pour some water and get started right away.

Minimalism saves you time, and more time saved means less time working and more free time to enjoy.

I KNOW many people are tired of hearing preaching about minimalism, but I wouldn't preach to you about it if it weren't a powerful way to increase your productivity.

In the next chapter, I'll take you through decluttering step by step to make it as easy as possible.

9

DECLUTTER YOUR SPACE

"You will find that it is necessary to let things go; simply for the reason that they are heavy. So let them go, let go of them. I tie no weights to my ankles."

C. JOYBELL C.

You do not have to downsize all at once. It would be easier if you did, but most people aren't comfortable with that. They spent a lot of time and money acquiring everything they own, and they don't want to throw away all that effort at once.

It's also challenging to do all at once. People new to minimalism often struggle to discern whether they should donate clothes they might fit into if they lose weight or whether they should donate sentimental gifts from ex-partners or old friends.

It is for this reason that organizing expert Marie Kondo recommends minimizing your possessions in a certain order:[1]

- Clothes

- Books
- Papers
- Miscellaneous Items
- Sentimental Items

The logic is this: Most people find it relatively easy to determine which clothes they want to keep versus donate. People find that decision harder to make for books, yet harder for papers, so on and so forth, with sentimental items coming in last. By the time you get to decluttering sentimental items, you are so practiced at judging your possessions that you are ready to make the difficult choices.

There are critics of Marie Kondo's method. Some people are righteously angry when she recommends they minimize their book collection. (Kondo believes that unless you are a voracious reader who is curating a library, you should own no more than thirty books.) Others think the Miscellaneous Items section should be broken out into kitchenware, home goods, and other subsections.

These criticisms miss the point. The magic of Marie Kondo's method isn't in any particular methodology. It's in her heuristic, her fundamental question:

Does this item spark joy?

If it does, keep it. If it doesn't, she says, toss it. Life is too short for anything else.

Clothes

The sad fact is that most Americans own far more clothes than they wear.

Take a look at the closet of an American. You will see a third of their clothes on the floor or in the laundry, a third of their clothes, and a third of their clothes shoved in the back of the closet.

The closet of a minimalist, on the other hand, does not have clothes strewn everywhere. All their clothes are either hung up or in the laundry bin. There are almost no clothes on the floor because there is plenty of space in the laundry bin and the closet. (The minimalist does not own enough clothes with which to cover their floor anyways.) There are no dressers with exploding drawers and bins squirreled under beds. Every article of clothing the minimalist owns gets worn.

The aspiring minimalist's goal is to get as close to this ideal as possible.

The best place to start is with any storage bins you may have. The next best place to start is in the back of your closet, where all the forgotten clothes have gone to hide.

Marie Kondo also has one other technique I very much like: She recommends that when you minimize, you gather up every item you own in that category and put them all in the same place so you can see exactly how much you own.

When she does this with her clients, they are often rendered speechless by their towering piles of clothes. These piles can easily reach eight feet tall. We often own far more than we realize.

Books

I have an unpopular opinion about book ownership. I don't respect it.

When people tell me they "love books" or "love the smell of books" or "love the feel of paper in their hands," it is more likely to lower my opinion of them than raise it.

Why? Because most of the people I've met who say these things *aren't readers*.

Maybe they were once readers, perhaps in their childhood, but they haven't read a book cover-to-cover in years as adults. They like thinking of themselves as readers, not *being* readers.

Look, here's the deal. If someone told me they "love rock climbing" and showed me their collection of rock climbing equipment but hadn't been rock climbing in years, I'm not going to think they're into rock climbing. I'm going to think they are deluding themselves into thinking they are into rock climbing.

So it goes with books as well; if you own a bunch of books, but you don't read often, I think you're lying to yourself about being a "reader."

It's forgivable. People often want to think of themselves as "readers." "Readers" are "smart" and "readers" are "educated" and "readers" are... you get the idea. To think of oneself as a "reader" is to think of oneself in a very flattering light.

But there is a big difference between thinking yourself a reader and actually being one.

Coming back to owning books: owning books is wonderful if you're a reader. However, owning books is likely nothing more than an expensive attempt to prop up your self-image if you're not.

My recommendation for book ownership is to own no more than two times the amount of books you read in a year. If you read 50 books a year, that's 100 books in your library. If you read three books a year, that's six books on the shelf. This guideline gives you plenty of wiggle room to choose your next book without cluttering up your house with a personal delusion.

Papers

Unlike most of what we own, paperwork is purely practical. If we can't come up with a concrete reason to keep papers, they probably aren't worth keeping.

Which system of paperwork management is best for you is a topic long enough for its own chapter, so I'll simply share mine with you. Here is how I sort my paperwork:

- Keep: Anything for which the government requires me to keep a paper copy. So far, this includes my car title, my social security card, and my birth certificate.
- Scan: Anything I need to keep for personal records. This category contains receipts for auto work, copies of contracts, and certain financial documents.
- Recycle: Everything else. This category includes manuals for appliances, most receipts, and tons of other things most people think they should keep.

I have been filing my paperwork according to this method — in other words, recycling the vast majority of it — for years, and never once have I later needed something I've recycled. When I need paperwork, the company I need it from can always provide an up-to-date copy upon request.

Miscellany

Miscellany can be anything from kitchen appliances to a collection of video game equipment. Since there are dozens of different categories, I'll stick to those on which I have a considered opinion:

Kitchen Tools & Appliances

Many people have shelves and shelves full of kitchen equipment in their kitchens, pantries, and garages. Much of these kitchen accouterments are left to collect dust.

If your kitchen tools are building up dust, it's probably time to acknowledge you don't cook very much and just let it go. If you get interested in cooking again, you can buy an updated version of what you need later.

(And if you're worried about the cost of that: Every Goodwill I've ever been to has an overabundance of kitchen equipment, entire shelves dedicated to forks and spatulas and pots and pans and different kinds of toasters and vegetable steamers and dozens of other appliances I don't understand. If you live near a goodwill, you will never want for kitchen equipment.)

Technology

Ah, tech. How I love tech. If I ever get tens of thousands of dollars into credit card debt, it will be because I bought a bunch of tech.

I know I could because I see my friends do it: they own one, or two, or three tablets, and also a laptop and a desktop and a TV and a great monitor for their desktop that they keep next to the TV...

The best advice I can give on minimizing tech comes in two parts:

First, don't own duplicates. This advice applies mostly to rich people. If you own an iPhone Pro, sell the iPhone 8 that's collecting dust in your drawer. If you own more than one tablet, sell the ones you never seem to use. If you have multiple laptops, keep the one you take everywhere and sell the one you leave at home. And if you have more than one TV, then please, for the love of God, sell the second. No house needs more than one TV.

Second, don't spend money on features you don't need. Don't buy an iPhone 12 Pro unless you are a photographer. Don't buy a tablet if you're not going to use it at least 2 hours a day. Don't buy a smartwatch if you don't need a fitness tracker. You get the idea. Just get a basic phone and a base model laptop and be done with it. Many people waste thousands of dollars every year on state-of-the-art technology they never needed in the first place.

Furniture

Minimizing guides often overlook furniture, but furniture has a powerful effect on the way a home feels. A home with lots of furniture feels crowded, dark, and difficult to navigate. A home with the right amount of furniture feels comfortably open and relaxed. (A home with too little furniture, of course, feels like you haven't fully moved in.)

Benjamin Foley said it best: "No, I'm not suggesting you throw away your bed or your couch, but think long and hard if you need that 6th lamp or that 4th side table."

Are your small furniture pieces doing you any good? The side table you shoved in the corner in the kitchen — is it ever anything more than a landing zone for dirty dishes and trash? The stack of chairs taking up half the closet — do you ever actually get them out for guests? Or have they lived in the back of the closet for years?

Getting rid of these small pieces can open up a home very quickly.

Sentimental Items

When you classify something as sentimental, it has one purpose: to evoke a particular memory, be it a memory of a feeling or a day in your past.

To fulfill this function, you must *see* your sentimental item. You must view it or use it regularly.

Most people don't put sentimental items out where they can see them. They put them in cardboard boxes in the back of their closet.

A sentimental item in a cardboard box in the back of a closet not being used for its purpose is like every other item you own that you're not using for its intended purpose — *junk*.

As you go through your sentimental items, ask yourself what you want to do with this item.

- Do you want to display it on a shelf in your room?
- Do you want to use it until it falls apart?

- Do you want to get it a glass case or a frame so you may enjoy it?
- If you want to keep it in storage and view it only when you are in the mood, do you want to get a wooden storage box to store it mindfully?

Then there's the most important question of all: *Do you want to be reminded of what it reminds you of?*

When I thought about this for myself, I found most of the "sentimental" items I owned reminded me of things that, upon reflection, I didn't *want* to be reminded of.

Like my t-shirt with my middle school's name on it. It's not useful as a shirt because I don't want to wear a middle school t-shirt out and about, and it's not useful as a sentimental item because it doesn't "take me back" to anything (except how much growing up sucks). When I realized this, I pitched it and never regretted it.

On the other hand, we all own genuinely sentimental items — notes friends wrote as a child, photos of friends taken at parties — that we want to see. We can take these things out of storage and display them as reminders of what matters.

What to Do with What You're Donating

Some people get it into their heads that they will take all the stuff they're getting rid of to the appropriate donation facilities in a series of errands all over town.

I was one of those people. I tried to sell things on eBay or take them to donation facilities — anything but allowing them to end up in a landfill.

But after a few months of constant trips to different donation facilities, I realized a few things:

- I was sick of running errands
- Goodwill accepted everything I wanted to donate already
- The prospect of running these errands made tidying seem less appealing to me

Now, my strategy is simple. I take all items I can resell to resale shops. If the resale shop does not accept them, I take them directly to Goodwill.

Is Goodwill a problematic donation facility? Perhaps. But a problematic donation facility should have my clothes more than me.

NOW THAT YOU'VE decluttered your space, you're going to see a marked improvement in your ability to conduct your life.

But when it comes to the way you arrange your home, minimalism is just one piece of the puzzle. Minimalism helps you ensure you only own what you need, but after you do so, you need to make sure what you own is arranged to prioritizes your productivity and health.

That's called designing your space for flow, and it's what we're covering in the next chapter.

---

1. The Life-Changing Magic of Tidying Up by Marie Kondo (https://amzn.to/2GlDoKY)

10

DESIGN YOUR SPACE FOR FLOW

"Humans are built for flow. We just have to design our environment accordingly."

NIKLAS GÖKE

LIVING LIFE AS A HUMAN IS A LOT LIKE PLAYING A VIDEO GAME.

Consider an RPG video game. An RPG-style video game is nothing more than a series of artificial environments for the player.

Each environment presents the player with a set of options. The player can...

- Option A: Talk to an NPC
- Option B: Open doors, locks, or gates, and go to other areas
- Option C: Investigate the items in the area, pick them up, and use them

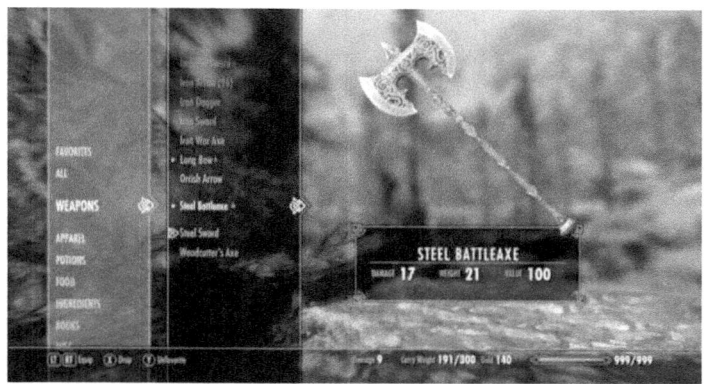

Screenshot of The Elder Scrolls: Skyrim

In real life, our options aren't constrained by what video game designers have decided for us.

But, like little video game designers, our brains constrain our options for us. When we walk into an environment, our brains generate a list of available choices, just like in a video game.

For instance, when someone walks into a living room with a couch, a TV, and a PS4, their brain generates a list of options that looks like this:

- Option A: Collapse on the couch and watch some Netflix
- Option B: Play some Far Cry
- Option C: Play some FIFA

When someone walks into a dirty kitchen with a sink full of unwashed dishes and a pantry full of unhealthy food, the options their mind generates look like this:

- Option A: Buy takeout

- Option B: Do the dishes
- Option C: Make some ramen

Choosing an option that is not on the brain's pre-generated list of options is challenging.

For instance, if you want to meal prep, but your kitchen is full of dirty dishes and unhealthy food, meal prepping involves cleaning your entire kitchen and going to the store, and that's before even *starting* to make the food.

The list of options the brain generates is not rational. The brain does not base this list on what's possible, our goals, or even what we want. The brain bases its list on immediately available and what's immediately pleasurable and almost nothing else.

Our brains do this because they didn't evolve for rationality and long-term thinking. Our brains evolved to help us survive on a moment-to-moment basis in a harsh, competitive natural environment.

As Richard Dawkins explains in *The Selfish Gene*, the evolutionary process prioritizes what allows an organism to survive and reproduce in a harsh and competitive natural environment. In the case of early humans, that meant prioritizing short-term thinking and pleasure associated with reproduction.

That's great for helping primitive humans make more little humans and put on fat for the winter, but it isn't great for helping modern humans lose that extra fifteen pounds or save money for retirement. When it comes to these goals, evolution screwed us.

THE GOOD NEWS is that we can do something in real life we can't do in a video game: *modify our environment.*

In a video game, you're stuck with what the video game designers have given you. But in real life, you're able to make changes to your environment that change the list of options your brain generates.

For instance, consider the kitchen example given above. Our protagonist's kitchen has a sink full of dirty dishes and a pantry with unhealthy food options, so her brain generates options like "make ramen" and "clean the kitchen." But what if the kitchen had clean dishes put away and healthy food in the pantry and fridge? Her options would look more like...

- Option A: Cook a quinoa bowl
- Option B: Have some soup
- Option C: Meal prep for the next few days

Now *those* are some options I can get behind.

UNDERSTANDING the concept of environmental options is crucial for understanding how to get into a flow state.

The ability to enter a flow state is predicated on two things:

- The ability to enter a flow state
- The ability to remain in a flow state

Both of those things are dependent on your environment. The harder your environment makes it for you to enter a flow state, the less likely you will. And the harder your environment makes it for you to remain in one, the shorter your periods of flow state will be.

To maximize our periods of flow, we need to design environments that:

- Give us the best choices for what to do
- Allow us to focus on what we're doing once we've chosen

How to Design Your Environment for Flow

First, decide on your goals. The first step to designing your environment is deciding what you want out of your environment. Marie Kondo calls this "setting an intention." Other people like to attach numbers to it and call it "goal setting."

I like to start by doing this at a macro level, deciding what my intentions are for not just one environment but also my entire life.

For example, the intentions I've set right now for my life are, loosely:

- To write, submit, and publish more articles
- To read books and Medium articles
- To exercise and stretch regularly
- To meditate daily
- To avoid getting high or drinking alcohol

This list determines the priorities for the environments in my life.

Second, design your environment around your intentions. You want to create an environment that makes it *easy* for you to act on your intentions and *difficult* to do otherwise.

For instance, one of my intentions in April 2019 was to give up watching TV. At the time, I lived in my parents' house, and I'd arranged my bedroom with one empty white wall for my projector TV to project on.

Thanks to this environment, it was very tempting for me to come home from work and collapse on my bed, zonked out in front of a wall-sized television.

To make my dream of giving up TV come true, I had to do something painful: sell the projector TV.

The projector TV was awesome. It was only $600, and it made your $3000 ULED flatscreen look like a stupid toy. I did *not* want to sell it. But someone who doesn't watch TV doesn't need a TV, no matter how awesome it is. I was trying to become someone who doesn't watch TV, so it had to go.

And just like that, I achieved my goal. In May of 2019, I watched less than five hours of TV.

Most environmental interventions are not that obvious or easy to make, but they're there. For example...

- If one of your intentions is to have better sex with your partner more frequently, there's lots of evidence to suggest getting rid of the TV in your bedroom is the way to do so.[1]
- If one of your intentions is to eat more home-cooked meals, refuse to buy snacks and instant-ready meals so your environment forces you to cook.

- If one of your intentions is to meditate daily, buy a meditation cushion and set it out in a specific spot to remind you to meditate whenever you see it.

Ask yourself: does my home make it easy to do what I want to be doing?

Chances are it does not. Most Americans arrange their home so the living room has a couch and multiple chairs which face a TV. The desks and bookshelves are frequently an afterthought, stuffed into an alcove or bedroom corner. They shove their home gym equipment into a drawer in the coffee table, and they display their alcohol proudly on a visible shelf.

What stops most people from achieving what they want to achieve is not a lack of ability or laziness, but merely the things that make them stumble; the fact that they'd have to clean their kitchen and go grocery shopping to meal prep, or that they'd have to rearrange all their furniture to do some at-home exercises.

Environmental design is powerful precisely because it removes these roadblocks. It's a lot easier to walk down a paved road on a sunny day than it is a rocky path in the middle of a rainstorm, and it's a lot easier to be productive and make healthy choices when you don't have to fight a torrent of clutter and undone tasks.

My challenge to you is this: take an honest look at your life and ask yourself how your environment affects your ability to enter flow. Are your home, office, and digital environments designed to maximize your ability to do what you want? Or are they filled with clutter and distractions? You can achieve your goals either way, but one way makes it that much harder.

THAT BRINGS us to the end of what you can do for your physical space. But in the modern age, our physical space is only one piece of the productivity puzzle. Just as important as our physical space is our digital space, the environment we're in when we use our computers, phones, and tablets.

The rest of this book is dedicated to helping you optimize your digital space for productivity and flow, starting in the next chapter with your email.

---

1. https://www.brides.com/story/having-a-tv-in-bedroom

11

GET TO INBOX ZERO

"It's about how to reclaim your email, your attention, and your life. That "zero?" It's not how many messages are in your inbox–it's how much of your own brain is in that inbox. Especially when you don't want it to be. That's it."

MERLIN MANN, FOUNDER OF THE INBOX
ZERO MOVEMENT

SINCE YOU INSTALLED TIME TRACKERS, YOUR COMPUTER AND mobile devices are hard at work tracking how much time you spend on your digital devices.

Those trackers aren't done collecting data yet, but I'm willing to bet that you wish you spent less time on email no matter what the results are.

Why? Nobody likes email, that's why.

So what we're going to work on today is helping you spend less time checking it.

There are a lot of strategies out there for managing email. Some people say you should only check your email twice a day. Others say you should categorize, archive, and organize your emails a particular way. Others still treat their email as a stream-of-consciousness feed of notifications.

All these strategies miss the point. They're just alternative ways to deal with all the emails you get.

You don't need new strategies to deal with the emails you get -- you need to get **fewer emails.**

Types of emails we get that we don't need to get include:

- Advertising mailing lists. What happens is the marketing professionals at large companies get a hold of your email address, and they use it to send you advertisements. Or you sign up for them yourselves so you can get a free discount, coupon, or some other benefit. And instead of unsubscribing, we allow these emails to pile up in our inbox.
- Notification emails. Every time we download a new app or make a new account on a website, that software signs us up for notifications. So every time something happens on that platform, we get an email about it. These emails jam up inboxes and make them impossible to navigate.
- Spam. Many people think spam is just a fact of the universe, but the reality is that you can unsubscribe from spam most of the time. It's against the law to send emails to lists without an unsubscribe button, so if you look for the unsubscribe button at the bottom of your spam emails, you can get off those lists.

The good news is, it's easy to get fewer emails. Here's what you have to do:

1. Open your inbox.
2. Identify one email that comes from a mailing list.
3. Scroll to the bottom, find the "unsubscribe" button, and click unsubscribe.
4. Go back to your inbox. Search for all emails from that sender.
5. Delete them all.
6. Go back to step one.

Depending on how cluttered your email inbox is, this can take several hours. But once it's done, you never need to do it again. You'll have fewer emails to deal with, forever.

YOU MAY FIND it's difficult for you to unsubscribe from some of these newsletters. If that happens, ask yourself these questions:

1. When was the last time I read or used an email from this sender? If the answer is "over seven days ago," unsubscribe. You're not reading these emails, you're just deluding yourself into thinking you do.
2. Refer back to your priority list. Does this email support one of your stated priorities? If not, unsubscribe.

These rules may feel ruthless. That's because they are. As we discussed, when setting priorities, productivity takes focus. You don't just need to say "yes" to what you want, you need to say "no" to everything else — and that includes spending your time reading emails.

CONGRATULATIONS! You've made a lot of progress cleaning out your email inbox today. But more importantly, by unsubscribing from emails, you've made sure your email inbox is going to *stay* clean. This change will help you be productive far into the future.

Your email, however, is just one piece of your digital space. Another element that is just as important is your smartphone. In the next chapter, you will learn how to break your phone addiction and optimize your phone for productivity.

12

BREAK YOUR PHONE ADDICTION

> "The tycoons of social media have to stop pretending that they're friendly nerd gods building a better world and admit they're just tobacco farmers in t-shirts, selling an addictive product to children. Because let's face it, checking your likes is the new smoking."
>
> BILL MAHER

ONE OF THE BIGGEST IMPEDIMENTS TO YOUR PRODUCTIVITY IS right next to you. It might be sitting on a desk, lying on a bed, or even in your hand right now.

Can you guess what it is?

Your phone.

The vast majority of the time you're using your phone, it's an obstacle to your productivity. It's taking your focus away from what you want to be doing and redirecting it to an app.

This redirection is no accident. Software developers have been for a decade perfecting the art of creating apps that divert you from what you're doing to give their software your attention. Nearly everyone who is not conscientious about their phone use has allowed software developers to colonize their free time.

Let's find out if you have too.

Earlier in the course of this book, you installed time trackers on your computers and phones. Well, go ahead and check those phone trackers now.

If you forget how, here are the links:

- Screen Time (iPhone): https://support.apple.com/en-us/HT208982
- Google Digital Wellbeing (Android): https://support.google.com/pixelphone/answer/9137850

Do you like what you see?

———

BEFORE WE GET STARTED BREAKING your phone addiction, I'd like to give you two reassurances about my strategy for helping you break your phone addiction:

1. I will not recommend you delete any of your apps. You can keep your social media, games, and everything else you want to use. The problem isn't that these things exist, but how you configure your phone to allow them to dominate your attention.
2. I will not recommend you set use timers, downtime hours, or other parental-control-style interventions. You don't need more self-control, you need a phone that doesn't make you exert it in the first place.

So let's get started.

Step 0: Defining Phone Addiction

Before you can break your addiction to your phone, you need to understand what it means to be addicted to your phone.

We call it a "phone addiction," but you're not addicted to your phone. If your phone was the problem, you could throw your phone in the trash and be done with it. What you're addicted to is *the apps on* your phone.

There are two categories the apps on your phone fall into:

1. Healthy apps

2. Addictive apps

When an app is healthy for you, it makes your life better. You don't feel a compulsion to use it. You use it when you need it, and the rest of the time, you don't even think about it. Using them makes your life better.

Healthy apps typically include the basics, like your banking apps, calculator, phone, calendar, map, etc. They also include educational apps, apps that help you relax, meditating apps, study apps, and any other app that makes your life healthier and happier.

Addictive apps are the opposite. You feel a compulsion to use them many times a day. They make you feel bad after you use them. Using them holds you back.

Addictive apps encompass nearly all social media, all phone games that are not educational (especially those with in-app purchases), and real-time news apps, for starters. Almost any app can be an addicting one if it is creating a problem for you.

You need to figure out which apps are addictive for *you*.

Refer back to your priorities for your life. Now, look at your statistics for your phone use. Which apps are you using a lot that support your goals, and which apps are you using a lot that keeps you from your goals?

I'm going to make a few assumptions about your priorities. I assume your priorities did NOT include...

1. Using social media more
2. Playing more phone games
3. Checking the news more often
4. Checking your email more often
5. Getting lost in feeds more often

These assumptions won't be correct for everyone, of course. But the majority of people who are interested in breaking phone addictions find the above behaviors to be a problem for them.

So, as we proceed through this chapter, eliminating these will be a priority.

Once it's clear which apps are healthy and addicting for you, move on to the next step.

For more information about why social media is addictive, watch the Netflix documentary The Social Dilemma.

Step 1: Delete Apps You Don't Use

There's no point in reorganizing and optimizing apps you don't need, so the first step is to delete apps you don't need.

If there are any apps you don't use on your phone, delete them.

Maybe you had plans to use this app in the future, or perhaps you used to use them, but now you don't. Regardless of how you got the app, if you don't use it, it's got to go.

Deleting apps you don't use may seem like a simple step. It is, but the next few sections require a lot of configuring, and it will save you a lot of time if you delete apps you aren't using anyway.

Step 2: Turn off Notifications and Badges

The most important thing you can do to break your phone addiction is to turn off those damned notifications and badges.

Perhaps *the* most addicting parts of your phone is your phone's notifications. Software engineers design them to grab your attention and *not let go*. Using well-researched psychology principles, they create notifications that are as enticing as the smell of free freshly-baked cookies.

And it works. Once we see them, we almost always swipe. Whatever we were doing is interrupted, and the notification leads us off-track into a new activity.

The best way to combat this is not to see them in the first place.

Turning off notifications doesn't mean you don't get to use those apps. It just means those apps don't have permission to interrupt you while you're trying to live your life.

My rule of thumb is that you should turn off any notifications except those from a real human trying to contact you personally. So after you turn off all your notifications, you should only be getting...

1. Texts, phone calls, or direct messages
2. Social media posts in which someone tagged you
3. Phone system notifications

And that's it!

Examples of the kinds of notifications you *shouldn't* be getting include...

- Any single-player game notifications.
- Any Facebook notification that isn't someone telling you something. This kind includes 'happening near you,' 'your friend liked this page,' and 'your friend posted a commend on your other friend's status.' If the notification doesn't have your name, get rid of it.
- Notifications for Snapchat stories. If you want to check your friend's stories, you can, but your phone doesn't get to interrupt you to tell you about it.
- Any notifications which tell you someone is going online
- Any notifications which invite you to "go online."
- Any notifications that start with "it's been a while since..."

You should also turn off your email notifications. Software designers created email for messages which aren't urgent. Most people get a lot of emails every day - don't permit these emails to interrupt you.

How to turn off notifications:

There are two ways: at the app level and the system level.

Start at the app level. To do this, open the app for which you want to turn off notifications. Go to settings and find the section called "notifications." Turn off all the notifications that don't directly mention you, as described above.

Here are some links on how to do this for common apps:

- The Facebook notifications preferences page[1]
- Snapchat notifications how-to: iOS[2], Android[3]
- Twitter how-to page for managing mobile notifications[4]

If there are no app-level notification preferences (as there won't be for some apps), go to the system level and turn notifications off there.

Here are some customer support articles on how to do this for iOS and Android:

- Turning notifications off on iOS[5]
- Turning notifications off on Android[6]

Next, we're going to work on replacing your bad habit of using addicting apps with good ones.

For extra credit, turn off all of your social media notifications on your phone. Get rid of any notifications that don't have anything to do with you, and reroute the ones addressed to you personally to your email. That way, you check them when you want, not when your phone wants.

Step 3: Download Some Healthy Apps

A lot of digital decluttering experts recommend deleting all your apps cold-turkey. But when I was first starting to break my phone dependency, that advice never worked for me. I'd go to the BMV and have to wait in line, or be sitting in a doctor's office, and inevitably end up redownloading all the apps I told myself I didn't want to use. Without something else to occupy me, I went right back to my bad habits.

What eventually worked for me was *positive habit replacement*.

Positive habit replacement is the term psychologists use for replacing a bad habit with a good one. For instance, if you have a nasty habit of chewing your nails, positive habit replacement would mean replacing the habit of chewing your nails with the habit of taking a deep breath to relax.

If you're addicted to your phone, you have a nasty habit of using unhealthy apps when you pull out your phone. I certainly did. The positive habit I used to replace this bad habit was playing educational apps.

Whenever I pulled out my phone habitually, I didn't force myself to put it away. I played Duolingo to teach myself Spanish. Instead of wasting my time on endless social media, I started to learn a second language!

After a few weeks, I broke my addiction to social media, thanks to Duolingo. When I did delete my social media apps off my phone, I never downloaded them again, thanks to Duolingo.

The best part is, I never got addicted to Duolingo. Educational games are healthy, not addicting, so it was easy to stop playing Duolingo when I wanted.

And like that, with no special effort on my part, my phone addiction was broken.

Do the same for yourself. Find some educational apps and games you enjoy using and put them on your home screen.

There are a lot of options from which you can choose.

- **Duolingo.** Duolingo a free app that teaches you another language. It uses the same techniques that make social media addictive and fun to make learning another language addictive and fun.
- **Kindle.** So many people claim they want to read more. Well, it's a lot easier to read more if your books are always with you.
- **Brilliant.** Brilliant is an app that uses the same addictive app concepts to teach people math, science, engineering, and other practical skills.
- **Mimo.** Mimo is a great app to get started learning to code. You could also try ProgrammingHub.
- **Elevate.** Elevate trains your brain to be more effective at basic skills. After using Elevate, I noticed my ability to do mental math and read short text sections went way up.

If there are any skills you particularly want to learn, you can also search the app store or play store and find apps that teach you those skills.

Download some of these apps and play with them. Decide which ones you like the most, and put them on your home screen.

There's just one thing you need to know.

Educational apps are not usually free.

The reason is that an app can only be free when *you are the product*, such as when Facebook gets you addicted to the feed so they can show you ads.

With educational apps, you are not the product. Knowledge is the product, which they are selling to you. As a result, they are not free. And that's a good thing. It means you're their number one priority -- not an advertiser.

So, if you want to break your phone addiction, you'll need to get into the habit of paying for apps.

That may feel expensive, but here's a little perspective: That's the cost of takeout one time per month. I know you buy takeout more than once a month, so don't tell me you don't have the money. And unlike takeout, these apps will make your life a lot better.

Next, we're going to work on rearranging your apps, so you never see your addicting apps again.

Step 4: Rearrange Your Apps on Your Home Screen

Most people have their phones organized, at least according to them. If you ask them if their home screen is organized, they will tell you it is.

But *I'm* telling you, the way most people organize their phone is garbage.

Think of the pages of your phone like a menu. Each app is an activity you can pick. Some are full, healthy meals, like educational games, and others are deep-fried dessert, like social media.

You want to pick healthy options, right?

The best way to do this is to design a menu that encourages you to pick healthy options. One does this by putting healthy choices on the home screen and making addicting ones hard to access.

Most people's phone organization is garbage because they don't do this. They put addicting choices front and center. Then they're surprised when they end up addicted to their phone.

Ever hear the phrase *out of sight, out of mind?* You're going to put your addicting apps out of sight.

As of iOS 14, both iOS and Android both have fully configurable home screens. The ability to configure your home screen means you can pick which apps appear on the home screen and hidden in the app library. (You can also select widgets for your home screens, but we will not worry about those).

The first step is to pick 5-10 apps that you want yourself to use. Include your educational apps here.

The second step is to move those all to your home screen.

The third step is to delete every other app icon and widget.

I'm serious. Delete every other app icon on your phone. Everything that's in a group, everything that's got its own special page, everything that you've put into some clever organizational system, delete them all.

By the end of this process, you should have only *one* home screen. No exceptions.

Now, when you pick up your phone, you're only going to see healthy apps you want to use. The rest of your apps are out of sight.

If you want to access an out-of-sight app, use your phone's search function.

Here's how:

- iOS Search Function: https://support.apple.com/en-us/HT211345
- Android Search Function: https://support.google.com/android/answer/9079646?hl=en

This system's beauty is that by being forced to find the app you want, you can only use apps you consciously choose to use. You can't use an app out of habit.

You use apps when *you* choose, not when your phone chooses.

―――――

I KNOW these changes feel strange. They may even be a little anxiety-inducing. You may feel afraid of missing something. But don't worry. What's happening is the opposite -- you're clearing out what isn't essential to make room for what is.

Now that you've taken the big step of optimizing your phone, next up is your computer.

―――――――――――――――――――

1. https://www.facebook.com/settings?tab=notifications
2. https://support.snapchat.com/en-US/a/ios-notifications
3. https://support.snapchat.com/en-US/a/android-notifications
4. https://help.twitter.com/en/managing-your-account/notifications-on-mobile-devices
5. https://support.apple.com/en-us/HT201925
6. https://support.google.com/android/answer/9079661?hl=en

13

OPTIMIZE YOUR COMPUTER

> "I think it's fair to say that personal computers have become the most empowering tool we've ever created. They're tools of communication, they're tools of creativity, and they can be shaped by their user."
>
> BILL GATES

YOUR PHONE IS OFTEN THE BIGGEST IMPEDIMENT TO YOUR productivity, but the most significant *opportunity* you have to increase your productivity is your computer.

Everyone has something important they do with their computer. Students use it to research and do classwork, white-collar workers perform their jobs on their computer (and so do many blue-collar workers), and even retirees use their computers to pay bills and pursue hobbies. Your computer is so critical to your workflow that I've included this entire chapter on optimizing it for productivity.

The first thing to do is, like with your phone, check the time tracker you installed earlier — in this case, RescueTime. See what RescueTime has to say about your computer use.

Do you like what you see?

Unlike phone use, which you should keep to a minimum for mental health reasons, there's no "ideal" amount of computer use. All you want to do is make sure your "unproductive" time doesn't rise above six or seven hours a day -- in other words, you want to make sure it doesn't get out of control.

To that end, let's go over some ways you can optimize your computer for fast and productive work sessions:

Set up and Use Cloud Storage

The four most popular cloud storage solutions are Apple iCloud, Microsoft OneDrive, Google Drive, and Dropbox. I use a privacy-oriented service called Sync. Pick the one that looks best for you and move *all* your files into it.

You should have nothing hanging around on your Desktop or in your Documents, Downloads, or in any other weird folders when you're done. It should all be stored safely in the cloud.

Why store everything in the cloud?

When you store everything in the cloud, you don't need to worry about your computer breaking. I could drop my laptop in the toilet right this second, and I wouldn't lose any data because I store all my files on Sync.

Storing everything on Sync also makes it easy to find everything because I always know where it is — Sync. If I ever have trouble finding anything, all I need to do is navigate to Sync, open the search bar, and type in search terms until it pops up.

Learn to Touch Type

The most common obstacle to productivity that people have on the computer is typing slowly.

Most people type at a rate of roughly 30 words per minute. They use three or four fingers on each hand, each with their own idiosyncratic way of typing.

Professional typists don't type in their own idiosyncratic way. They type using the Touch Typing method, a typing method that involves using all of your fingers on each hand. And this method works; touch typists type at a blistering rate of 90 to 110 words per minute.

Do the math. If you currently type at 30 words per minute and learn to type at 90 words per minute, you can triple your typing speed.

How much more could you get done if you could type *three times as fast*?

The best part is, it only takes two weeks to learn. Go to typingclub.com, sign up for a free account, and spend an hour or two a day taking their typing lessons. After two weeks, you'll be typing at close to 80 words per minute. How's that for productivity?

A word of warning: Once you start practicing touch typing, your typing efficiency will go down for a week or two as you struggle to unlearn your old habits of typing and replace them with new ones. Don't be discouraged; pushing through this slump is well worth it.

Learn to Use Keyboard Shortcuts

Once you've learned to type correctly, you can learn the second secret of computer productivity -- using keyboard shortcuts.

If someone told me I could only navigate my computer using its cursor, I'd go nuts. Using the mouse and clicking takes forever. Navigating by keyboard shortcut is *so* much faster. Like typing properly, it can shave hours off of your week.

On my Macbook, I rely on a caché of keyboard shortcuts:

- Command (⌘) + Space for Spotlight
- Command (⌘) + Tab for switching applications
- Command (⌘) + Q for quitting applications
- Command (⌘) + W for closing the currently open window
- Command (⌘) + A for "select all"
- Command (⌘) + F for "find"
- Command (⌘) + Z for "undo"
- Command (⌘) + S for "save"
- Command (⌘) + C for "copy"
- Command (⌘) + V for "paste"
- Command (⌘) + N for opening a new window
- Command (⌘) + Shift + N for creating a new folder
- Command (⌘) + P for "print"
- Enter allows you to change a file or folder name while it is selected
- Command (⌘) + 1, 2, 3, etc for tab switching
- Command (⌘) + T for opening a new tab
- Command (⌘) + L for selecting the browser URL field

- Option + Arrow Keys for jumping to the next or previous word in a text field

These are the keyboard shortcuts for Mac, but they're nearly identical for Windows. To use shortcuts on windows, substitute CTRL for ⌘.

Learn to Use the Search Function

Once you can type correctly and use keyboard shortcuts, you can start taking advantage of computers' search function.

Most people try to find applications by scrolling, clicking, and looking around their computer, but using the search function is an exponentially faster way of navigating your machine.

On Mac, the search function is called Spotlight. Spotlight is easy to use. Press Command (⌘) and Space at the same time, and it will pop up. Type in the name of any application, file, folder, song, photo, or any other thing you are looking for, and your Mac will deliver it right to your screen.

On Windows, it's even easier. Press the Windows key on your keyboard, and the search window will pop up. Type in your search terms, whether that be an application, file, or website, and it will pop up here.

LEARNING how to navigate your computer quickly is a potent productivity habit. That being said, most people do everything they do on their computer in their browser. So, your last productivity lesson will be on optimizing your browser, which begins in the next chapter.

14

OPTIMIZE YOUR BROWSER

"If I were to wish for two things, they would be as much bandwidth as possible and ridiculously fast browser engines."

MATT MULLENWEG

IN THE LAST CHAPTER, WE WORKED TOGETHER TO OPTIMIZE your computer experience. But the most used part of your computer is your browser, so I want to take some time to talk about it in particular.

Most people I've met use their browser haphazardly. They have ten, a hundred, a thousand tabs open at once, each with its own thing loaded and waiting to play. Most people also have several dozen browser extensions, each bouncing with its own thing.

Using your browser this way splits your focus, makes your computer a noise machine, and makes it slow. What you need to do is get your browser under control.

Here's how:

Get Rid of All Your Tabs

When it comes to tabs, I do something many people don't do: *I close out of every tab and quit my browser at the end of every browsing session.* At the start of every new browsing session, I start with one empty tab.

(In fact, I quit *all* applications before shutting my laptop lid. Whenever I open my laptop, I open it to a clean desktop and no applications.)

I imagine people find it difficult to close out of all their tabs for the same reason they find it difficult to get to inbox zero or quit side-projects that are going nowhere: they are unable to admit to themselves what they are or aren't going to do. Each open tab is a to-do; "I'm going to read this article," "I'm going to take action on this form," so on and so forth.

It's time for you to admit to yourself you are never going to look at those tabs. The key to focus and productivity across the board, computer or no computer, is learning to identify what you do and don't need to do in the first place.

So go ahead and do it now. Close out of all your tabs.

Once that's done, change your browser settings so that your browser always starts with a fresh slate. This configuration means that when your browser opens, it opens with one new, empty tab every time. Here's how to on Chrome,[1] Firefox,[2] and Safari.[3]

Download Some Useful Browser Extensions

Get rid of all your browser extensions. All of them.

Have you done that? Good.

Now here's what you should download:

- A password vault for saving passwords (such as LastPass or 1Password)
- Grammarly, to check your English as you type (not strictly productivity related, but will make your communication seem more professional)
- An ad blocker, because ads are bad for your sanity
- Pocket, an extension for saving articles, so you can save pages here instead of opening new tabs

This configuration is what I use for my browser. Here is a complete list of every extension I use:

- **1Password:** To connect to my 1Password vault, which syncs across all my devices.
- **Pocket:** To save articles that seem interesting into a list of articles I will probably never read.
- **Honey:** To help me save money when I make online purchases
- **Grammarly for Chrome:** The joy of good grammar, everywhere I am on the internet.
- **uBlock — free ad blocker:** In addition to blocking ads across the internet, I've specifically configured uBlock to block Mint's incessant free credit card offers. Mint is an excellent service, but the constant credit card offers drive me bonkers.

You'll notice there are no distraction blockers (SelfControl, StayFocused, etc.) on this list. I don't believe in time-restricted content blockers because I think if something's bad for you, it's bad for you *all* the time, not just some of the time. If there's something I think I need to restrict myself from, I restrict myself from it across the board. This policy has helped my productivity far more than any distraction blockers ever have.

Learn to Use Bookmarks

Most people use the bookmarks section of their browser haphazardly, more as a place to store cool links when they come across something cool they want to save rather than a real productivity tool.

This use case is not what software engineers had in mind when they designed bookmarks. Engineers meant bookmarks to be places where you save links to websites you need to visit frequently. That's why they occupy valuable space right underneath the URL bar on your browser.

If you're not clicking on a bookmark at least once a week, you shouldn't bother having that website bookmarked at all.

You should make a list of the ten websites you visit the most (or *should* visit the most, at least) and create bookmarks for those.

This advice probably seems like pretty annoying, basic stuff. But going through your computer and taking the time to make sure you configure your settings correctly can save you dozens of hours of technological struggle over a year of work — or if you're using an old computer, days.

---

1. https://support.google.com/chrome/answer/95314?hl=en
2. https://support.mozilla.org/en-US/kb/change-homepage-specific-page
3. https://support.apple.com/en-us/HT204296

CONCLUSION

You've reached the end of *Work Less, Finish More!*

You should feel proud of yourself. If you've implemented all the changes in this book as you read, you'll notice your productivity significantly increasing without any special effort or exercise of willpower on your part. Instead of struggling with motivation and forcing yourself to be productive, your productivity will naturally rise with each day.

So get out there, spend less time working, and start enjoying all the free time you have on your hands.

LIKED THE BOOK? LEAVE A REVIEW!

If you enjoyed *Work Less, Finish More,* or found anything within it helpful, please consider leaving a review.

Reviews are crucial to a book's success on the Amazon store. Without reviews, books are destined to not sell. But only a fraction of readers decide to leave one. It would be immensely helpful if you were one of them.

I read every review. Your review is not only important to me because it helps me sell books, it's also crucial feedback for me. I worked hard on this book and want to make sure it fulfilled every expectation you had.

I want *Work Less, Finish More* to help as many people as possible. That won't happen without your review.

Follow this link to leave a review:
http://www.amazon.com/review/create-review?&asin=B08M2QNLLK

GET SEEKING TRUTH

It's the end of the book, but it doesn't have to be the end of our conversation. You can keep in touch with me by signing up for my weekly newsletter Seeking Truth.

> "Thank you for all of the articles that you share... I am SO looking forward to being in bed tonight and getting a chance to read this latest installment. I want to read all of the stories this time!"
>
> JACQUIE

Sign up for Seeking Truth here:
https://www.meganeholstein.com/join/

Seeking Truth includes:

1. Thoughts and a quote for the coming week
2. A summary of every article I wrote that week
3. Book and article recommendations for the week

Why else should you sign up for Seeking Truth

- Have something to say? Reply to the digest and let me know.
- I write articles by request – it's like having your own personal researcher. Email me the topic you'd like to know more about, and I'll write about it.

Sign up for Seeking Truth here:
https://www.meganeholstein.com/join/

ABOUT THE AUTHOR

Megan Holstein is a personal growth blogger whose work has been read over four million times. She's published author of *Work Less, Finish More: Productivity Lessons on How to Spend Less Time Working* and *Get More Done and iPhone App Design for Entrepreneurs: Find Success on the App Store without Coding*. She is a top writer on Medium where over 18,000 people have subscribed to her work. Over 3,500 people read her weekly newsletter Seeking Truth.

Prior to becoming a writer, Megan Holstein was an entrepreneur. She was featured in Inc. Magazine as an award-winning college entrepreneur for the founding of Pufferfish Software, a company that made apps for autistic children. She won the YWCA woman to watch 2012 award and received a citation from Governor Kasich of the State of Ohio for her work with Pufferfish Software.

In her personal life, Megan enjoys hitting the gym, indoor gardening, reading over one hundred books a year, and not having to write biographies about herself in the third person.

www.ingramcontent.com/pod-product-compliance
Lightning Source LLC
Chambersburg PA
CBHW060842220526
45466CB00003B/1200